We Will Never Forget

We Will Never Forget

BELLEVUE UNIVERSITY

iUniverse, Inc.
Bloomington

We Will Never Forget

iUniverse books may be ordered through booksellers or by contacting:

iUniverse
1663 Liberty Drive
Bloomington, IN 47403
www.iuniverse.com
1-800-Authors (1-800-288-4677)

Because of the dynamic nature of the Internet, any web addresses or links contained in this book may have changed since publication and may no longer be valid. The views expressed in this work are solely those of the author and do not necessarily reflect the views of the publisher, and the publisher hereby disclaims any responsibility for them.

Any people depicted in stock imagery provided by Thinkstock are models, and such images are being used for illustrative purposes only.
Certain stock imagery © Thinkstock.

ISBN: 978-1-4759-7816-2 (sc)
ISBN: 978-1-4759-7817-9 (ebk)

Printed in the United States of America

iUniverse rev. date: 03/09/2013

Contents

Foreword

We will never forget . . .

The members of the United States military have built a tradition of honorable and faithful service. On the 10th anniversary of the September 11th terrorist attacks, Bellevue University initiated this book project to honor all veterans for their dedication to America and our freedom—and pay special tribute to the fallen patriots who made the ultimate sacrifice in defense of our liberty. They hold a cherished place in the history of the United States and in the memories of the people they served.

Today, all who wear the uniform of the United States are serving at a crucial hour in our history, and each has answered a great call to serve our nation on the front lines of freedom.

As our country continues to fight terrorism and promote peace and freedom, Bellevue University is proud to show its support of military personnel and their families by publishing "We Will Never Forget."

This book honors our soldiers who have fallen since Sept. 11, 2001, for their commitment to our country, and their legacy of patriotism and sacrifice. By giving their lives for the cause of freedom, these heroes have protected and inspired all Americans.

We feel it is a fitting tribute to those who made the ultimate sacrifice in service of our country, as well as their families and friends who mourn their passing and continue to feel the impact of their loss.

Located in Bellevue, Nebraska, the University was founded in part to support the educational needs of nearby Offutt Air Force Base, and has been a military-friendly institution for more than 40 years. Approximately 30 percent of students, faculty, and staff are military, former military, or military related.

We are very fortunate for our strong military ties and know our University is a better place because of the military personnel who have been part of our student body. In keeping with our tradition of providing military-friendly learning opportunities, we are pleased to donate the proceeds of this book to the National Military Family Association to fund military spouse scholarships.

We look forward to continuing our support of military personnel, as they continue to serve our great country.

Best regards,
Dr. Mary B. Hawkins
President, Bellevue University

Prologue

The images of September 11, 2001 are forever imprinted in our minds. Nearly 3,000 people lost their lives and new age of terrorism was born. More than a decade later, thousands more have sacrificed their lives as part of America's military response.

Today, all who wear the uniform of the United States Armed Services are serving at a crucial hour in our history, and each has answered a call to serve our nation on the front lines of freedom. The members of the United States military have built a tradition of honorable and faithful service. We honor all veterans for their dedication to America and our freedom—and this book pays special tribute to the fallen patriots who made the ultimate sacrifice serving Operation Iraqi Freedom and Operation Enduring Freedom. They hold a cherished place in the history of the United States and in the memories of the people they served.

This book features personal accounts shared by the families and friends of our fallen servicepersons.

Chapter 1

A through F

Memoirs of fallen soldiers listed alphabetically by last name

In Memory of Capt. Matthew Joseph August
2/19/1975-1/27/2004
One of three soldiers killed in a roadside bomb attack in Khalidiya, just east of Ramadi, Iraq, on January 27, 2004

Home City and State: North Kingstown, RI
Military Branch/Unit: Company B, 1st Engineer Battalion, 1st Brigade Combat Team, 1st Infantry Division, U.S. Army
Dates Served: 6/10/1993-1/27/2004
Tour of Duty: Operation Iraqi Freedom
Locations Served: USMA West Point, NY; Fort Benning, GA; Fort Riley, KS

Biography
Matthew August graduated in the United States Military Academy Class of 1997 and was commissioned in the Corps of Engineers. Ten years to the day after he took the oath of office on the Plain at West Point, he took command of "Bulldog" Company 1st Engineers at Fort Riley; they deployed to Iraq in September 2003.

On January 27, 2004, he led his company to investigate a report of a weapons cache. When the convoy arrived at the town of Khalidiya, it was hit by an improvised explosive device (IED), which knocked out Matthew's Humvee. As the engineers formed a security perimeter, another IED was detonated, followed by small-arms fire. Medics rushed to the burning Humvee and pulled out the occupants.

Matthew, his First Sergeant and driver were killed immediately. The gunner died two days later from his wounds. Matt's wife Maureen got a report at her office in Baghdad that a unit had been attacked with multiple casualties. She called Bulldog Company's headquarters and asked for the company commander. The person answering the phone was silent for a moment before saying, "Just a moment Ma'am." An officer came on the line and told Maureen that her husband was among the dead. Maureen said she only replied,

"No!" and hung up the phone. A few minutes later her battalion commander and a chaplain came to her and confirmed the report. They told her to gather a few things because she was going to be taken to the airport in Baghdad to escort her husband's body and those of the other men killed that day back to the United States.

Memories shared by Richard J. August, Proud Father

Matt was a good student who was satisfied with average or just above average grades. His mother and I would often find him "studying" on his bed with his eyes closed, book open across his chest. He would open one eye and say that he was "sharpening his ax." This referred to a fable I had told him about the woodsman who took frequent breaks, rested and sharpened his ax while his partner worked furiously all day chopping wood with a dull tool. Of course, at the end of the day the woodsman with a sharp ax cut more wood. Later, Matt's wife Maureen said this habit would drive her crazy when the two of them were studying together for their master's degrees at the University of Missouri. She would pull an "all-nighter" and Matt would "sharpen his ax." The next day their grades were usually similar. She said Matt told her his secret was to pay attention to the instructor during class.

An avid outdoorsman, Matt loved to hunt and fish. He got a determined look on his face when he saw trout or bass rising. Matt hunted pheasant, prairie chicken, ducks, deer, wild turkey and boar using bow and arrow, shotgun, black powder muzzle loader and rifle. He respected the game he hunted. On a Kansas duck hunting trip with me, Matt dropped a duck that fell in the swift current and floated away before we could reach it. I had to restrain him from wading out in the frigid water and risking his life to try to retrieve the duck.

In Memory of Staff Sgt. Timothy Louis Bowles
4/17/1984-3/15/2009
Killed along with three other soldiers when a roadside bomb exploded near their vehicle in the Bati Kot district of Nangarhar Province, Afghanistan

Home City and State: Tucson, AZ
Military Branch/Unit: 3rd Logistics Readiness Squadron, 3rd
   Mission Support Group, 3rd Wing, U.S. Air Force
Dates Served: 5/13/2003-3/15/2009
Tour of Duty: Operation Enduring Freedom
Locations Served: Cannon AFB, NM; Kunsan AB, Republic of
   Korea; Elmendorf AFB, AK

Biography
Staff Sergeant Timothy Louis Bowles was born on April 17, 1984
at Elmendorf AFB, Alaska. He grew up in Tucson, Arizona and
graduated from Tucson High School in 2002. He attended Pima
Community College before enlisting in the United States Air Force
as a Fire Truck Maintenance Technician on May 13, 2003. His first
assignment was to the 27th Logistics Readiness Squadron, Cannon
Air Force Base, New Mexico. He was assigned to Cannon from
December 2003 to July 2006. From July 2006 to July 2007, he was
reassigned to the 8th Logistics Readiness Squadron, Kunsan Air
Base, Republic of Korea. In July 2007, Timothy was reassigned to
the 3rd Logistics Readiness Squadron, Elmendorf Air Force Base,
Alaska.

In support of Operation Enduring Freedom, he volunteered to go
to Afghanistan as part of a Provision Reconstruction Team within
the Nangarhar Province. He deployed on November 1, 2008 and
was scheduled to remain in country for nine months. His duties
included maintaining the PRT vehicles on the base and on the
road. On some operations, he would pull double duty as vehicle
mechanic and dismounted security, and then return to the base and
repair vehicles to have them ready for the next day.

On March 15, 2009, Timothy was on a four-vehicle security patrol
to check on a local school site in Kot, Afghanistan. He was in an
armored Humvee with three Illinois Guardsmen when their vehicle
rolled over and detonated a pressure-sensitive bomb.

Memories shared by Louis G Bowles Jr., Proud Father, Master Sgt., U.S. Air Force, Retired

There are so many memories with Tim and not enough space to write them. One of our last memories was Mother's Day Weekend 2008. Timothy had arranged for us to fly out to California and meet him in Los Angeles (it was supposed to be a surprise for his mom). We spent a couple of days at Disneyland and California Adventure. It was just Timothy and us.

Another memory is in July 2007, Tim had returned from Korea and we went for a motorcycle ride one afternoon. The ride was cut short when my motorcycle broke; Tim had to go home, get the truck and haul me and the bike home.

In Memory of Hospitalman Dustin Burnett
8/17/1988-6/20/2008
Died during combat operations in Farah Province, Afghanistan

Home City and State: Bullhead City, AZ
Military Branch/Unit: Navy corpsman assigned to the 1st Marine
    Division
Tour of Duty: Operation Enduring Freedom

Dustin Burnett with mother Debbie and brother Devin.

Biography:
Dustin, a 19-year-old Navy Corpsman, was killed by a roadside bomb on Friday, June 20, 2008 in Afghanistan while fighting for our freedoms as section leader for 27 Marines in Operation Enduring Freedom. He was a Bullhead City local who attended Mohave High from 2002-2006. He played football for the Fort Mohave Thunderbirds all years.

After graduating high school, he joined the Navy and went off to war in Afghanistan. At a sendoff rally at the local American Legion Post, Bullhead City Mayor Jack Hakim presented Dustin with a key to the city. He served as a medic attached to a Marine division. He is survived by his mother and stepfather, and brother Devin.

Dustin Burnett with his father Donald.

Memories shared by Debbie Nuchols, Proud Mother

Dustin was my first born. He was the first person I loved more than I loved myself. Losing him was by far the hardest challenge I have faced in my very challenging life. As time goes by, I am blown away as I continue to learn how many people were touched by him during the short time he was in this world. I miss him so very much. He is my angel, my joy, my source of happiness, and my hero.

His dad (Donald) wanted everything for our kids to be just a little better than they were for us. Donald did not want Dustin to enlist; he wanted him to stay here so we could protect him. Dustin had another plan in mind—he wanted to protect us and our way of life.

For his brother, Devin, Dustin was the best big brother there could ever be. He was also a best friend. Devin looked up to Dustin like all little brothers do. But unlike some older brothers, Dustin took his responsibilities as a big brother with insightfulness and compassion.

For his friends, Dustin was always the "do-gooder" and defender of the weak. The most comforting memory I can think of is this . . . Two days after Dustin died, I received this letter from one of his friends:

> My friend Lindsay and I use to "fake argue" with "Texas" in one of our classes, pretty much every other day, LOL. Since he is Catholic and we are Protestants, Lindsay and I just didn't understand the whole "praying to everyone," which is a common question for those who aren't Catholics. I think it was a goal of his to make us understand, which is why it was never dropped. Anyway, whenever we had enough of "the argument," either Lindsay or I would ask Dustin, "Texas, who is your Lord and Savior?" He would answer, "Jesus Christ." And, if he had enough he would ask us the same . . . and that would be the end of the "fake argument" . . . until the next day!
>
> I'm reminded of John 14:6, "I am the way, the truth, and the life. No man comes to the Father but through me." "Texas" was such a good friend, and a believer in Christ. I know, for a fact, that I will see him again in Heaven one day.
>
> The pain of losing a child is something I would not wish upon my worst enemy. I feel like I have lost my biggest accomplishment in life. But, in this process and through all of this pain, I have had to realize that I am not the only one who lost Dustin. This town has lost a friend and the world has lost a hero. He will go on to touch as many people with his death as he did in his life. Dustin was compassionate, funny and insightful beyond his years. He was the champion for the right fight.

Dustin gave his life willingly and with full consent for each and every one of us. And, he gave his life with the same compassion and insight with which he lived his life. He was not tricked into his decision to enlist, and he could not have been swayed to change his mind.

Here's what I think he would have wanted us all to take away from this: He would have wanted this to bring something good. He would have wanted this to unite his community. He would have wanted this to spread love, not hate or anger—life is way too short for that. He would have wanted this to strengthen faith. And, he would have wanted us to be his champions for patriotism.

The following speech is from the movie, "Boondock Saints," Dustin's favorite movie. He made sure as many people to watched it as he could include, and he planned to have this speech put on him as a tattoo when he returned home; but, he never got the chance.

> Now you will receive us! We do not ask for your poor or
>   your hungry
>
> We do not want your tired or sick
> It is your corrupt we claim
> It is your evil that will be sought by us
> With every breath, we shall hunt them down
> Each day, we will spill their blood, 'till it rains down
>   from the skies!
>
> Do not kill, do not rape, do not steal.
> These are principles which every man, of every faith can
>   embrace.
> These are not polite suggestions.
> These are codes of behavior.
> And those of you that ignore them will pay the dearest
>   cost.
>
> There are varying degrees of evil.
> We urge your lesser forms of filth not to push the bounds
>   and cross over
> into true corruption . . . into our domain.
>
> But, if you do, one day you will look behind you,
> and you will see we three.
> And on that day, you will reap it!!

And we will send you to whatever God you wish.

And shepherds we shall be, for thee my Lord for thee,
Power hath descended forth from thy hand,
that our feet may swiftly carry out thy command,
We shall flow a river forth to thee,
and teeming with souls shall it ever be.
In nomine patris, et filiiet spiritus sancti.

When I raise my flashing sword,
and my hand takes hold on judgment,
I will take vengeance upon mine enemies,
and I will repay those who haze me.
Oh, Lord, raise me to Thy Right Hand and count me
among thy saints.

One last thing I would like to share is an assignment Dustin completed when he was 15 years old for his Confirmation class at St. Margaret Mary. Dustin was told to create a holy card for an uncanonized saint. The saint is not canonized because he is still alive—the saint is you. Here is the description and drawing of his saint:

I am the Patron Saint of the Armed Forces

I will uphold freedoms to people that have none. I seek out those that wish to bring hate and terror on my country because the majority of us worship you Lord. I am a soldier not only of the armed forces but of GOD.

I know this country is not perfect. But the United States of America is ours. As a nation, it belongs to us and, ultimately, it is what we make of it. Thank you to all of our fallen heroes—my son, and the sons and daughters of others, who have made this the beautiful nation it is today. Let's do our best to make sure they are never forgotten.

In Memory of Sgt. CAsey Byers
Killed by a makeshift bomb in Taqaddum, Iraq
8/3/1982-6/11/2005

Home City and State: Schleswig, Iowa
Military Branch/Unit: Company B, 224th Engineer Battalion,
    Iowa Army National Guard
Tour of Duty: Operation Iraqi Freedom

Casey Byers

Biography
Sgt. CAsey "THE" Byers was born three weeks late on August 3,
1982 in Clear Lake, California. Whenever his mother typed his
name, the A was capitalized, so that became how the family spelled
it. He enlisted in the Army National Guard when he was a junior
in high school. He completed half of his training his junior year
and graduated early so he could finish it his senior year. He went
to college full time and worked full time. He had an eye for detail.
The soldiers in his unit called him "eagle eyes" because he saw

things they never caught. He always had a smile on his face and he loved to be the center of attention. He had a knack for pushing your buttons—even if he didn't know you. He knew just what to do to get a rise out of someone.

Memories shared by Ann Byers, Proud Mother

I was seven to eight centimeters dilated with CAsey for three weeks. When my water broke we went to the local nine-bed hospital. They were full so they put me in a linen closet. I had CAsey within 10 minutes. We were able to take CAsey home shortly after birth that day and the medical staff came to our home.

CAsey was very athletic and slept very little. He had fiery red hair and even after several attempts to change the color, it returned to an orange tint. He was always laughing and smiling no matter his mood.

CAsey had a desire to be remembered, whether good or bad, after his death. He used to always say he was going to die early—before he was 25. He lived his life like there was no tomorrow. He was very active and believed: the more dangerous, the more intriguing.

Before CAsey left for Iraq, he made me promise 10 things if he did not come home. He made me promise to quit my job, travel and keep his daughter Hailey safe. He also made me promise that I would celebrate his life, not mourn his death, at his funeral. I was to relay to others, through my actions, how strong a person he was in his lifetime.

He also wanted me to bring his speed boat out into the middle of our acreage after the funeral. We were to sit in it and let people come in, one by one, to talk with us. We were to have a party and supply refreshments to all attending. After his funeral, we had about 200 people still at our home, sitting by our bonfire at 2 a.m. Ironically, this was the best day of my life. I found out so many neat things about CAsey; it helped us all mourn his death by telling stories and celebrating his life.

CAsey either called, wrote a letter, or e-mailed everyone who meant something to him the week before his death. He called me 45 minutes before his death to tell me he was not coming home and wanted to make sure I understood the 10 things I promised him. We cried and told each other how much we loved each other and how proud I was of him. He took a picture before he left on his mission and labeled it, "See Mom, I am okay and doing what I love." He wanted me to have a final picture of him. Before each mission, he took a picture and labeled it for me. I think the most ironic thing that happened after CAsey's death was when officials brought CAsey home to me after his cremation; the officer was crying. I relayed it is okay and he said, "No, you have to hear what happened at CAsey's cremation." The person thought the ashes had cooled enough and was sweeping the remains into the urn when the phone rang. When he came back from the phone call he found the broom had started on fire. CAsey's ashes had started the broom on fire. We laughed and cried because even after death, CAsey had the last word and was playing with fire.

CAsey has a daughter he has never met, as she was born while he was in Iraq. She lives with us, and looks and acts just like him. CAsey was very unique. One either loved or hated him; there was never any question how you felt. He had such a powerful imagination and, with no fear, he made life exciting. I am so proud of him. For some reason, I never gave CAsey a middle name. When he joined the Guard they told him he had to have a middle name. He refused to use initials so he made his middle name "THE." After that point, he went by The Byers. Never Byers, never CAsey, never CAsey Byers, but The Byers. He painted "The Byers" on roads, buildings, and bridges all over Iraq. Many soldiers have taken pictures of his name written throughout Iraq. Even today, I have people contact me to tell me how their lives have changed since knowing CAsey.

The last person to contact me decided to try CAsey's idea of doing contract work in Iraq. He did this and is now a physical trainer for the federal government. It was CAsey's constant pressure while he was alive that got this young man to decide it was time to get his life in order. He admits that without this, he would not be where he is today. He is so thankful CAsey was relentless when he was alive.

Every year our family gets together with CAsey's unit. It is always full of laughter and stories. He is buried in Arlington National Cemetery with his younger brother Justin Paul Byers, who after following in CAsey's footsteps and enlisting in the Army Reserves, was fatally hit by a truck days before CAsey's funeral in Iowa.

In Memory of Spc. Thomas Harold Byrd
8/4/1984-10/15/2005
One of five soldiers killed when a roadside bomb detonated near their M2A2 Bradley fighting vehicle during combat operations in Ramadi, Iraq

Home City and State: Tucson, AZ
Military Branch/Unit: Company A, 2nd Battalion, 69th Armor
Regiment, 3rd Brigade, 3rd Infantry Division, U.S. Army
Dates Served: 11/13/2003-10/15/2005
Tour of Duty: Operation Iraqi Freedom
Locations Served: Baqubah, Iraq; Ramadi, Iraq

Biography
Thomas was born at 11:57 a.m. on August 4, 1984 at St. Joseph's Hospital in Tucson. He was a native Arizonian and spent a majority of his childhood in Arizona. He was the first-born child, grandchild, great-grandchild and nephew. He was an active child who kept his family on their toes—they never knew what he was going to do.

He had a smile that could disarm anyone's bad mood, and he was admired by many. He could get anything with that smile.

He was a great son. He always treated everyone with respect. He loved to play practical jokes and surprise people.

He also played youth football, and spent one year in Pueblo, CO where he played high school football. The family returned to

Arizona in 2000. He attended Santa Rita High School for his sophomore, junior and senior years of high school. While a student there, he wrestled and took third place in the state tournament—he loved the sport.

Thomas joined the Army right out of high school. He left for boot camp in November of 2003. He was stationed at Fort Benning Army Base in Georgia, and he went to Iraq in January of 2005.

He is survived by many, including his grandmother, brother, aunts, cousins and many friends.

They call him their "Angel of Freedom."

Memories shared by Julia M. Byrd, Proud Mother

Thomas left us with many great memories—he was a force that people gravitated toward. I am so very proud of the man he was. Thomas was such a lively child that there was never a dull moment. He was always stirring the pot and causing good times. Here is just one favorite moment out of many:

Thomas surprised everyone when he came home for leave in August of 2005, just after his 21st birthday. He came home from Iraq with a smile on his face. He didn't let anything bring him down—even with the madness of the war and all he had seen. I was at work, standing with my back to the door, when he came in. My co-workers could see him and he signaled to them not to say anything. I stood there talking for a while before I turned around and saw my precious child standing there with the biggest smile on his face. I, of course, started crying and everyone in the room was smiling. I was speechless. It was so good to see him and hug him. It had been over eight months since I had seen him.

We went out for lunch and all I could do was smile and cry—I could barely eat. I returned to work after lunch, but I had to leave work because my head was in the clouds . . . high in the clouds. After that we surprised his Dad at an appointment he was attending. It was so much fun to see the smiles. My heart was so full of joy.

We had a party for him (that he did not want), but we had to have it anyway. I called him a hero and he said, "Mom, hero is for the fallen." Little did we know.

His smile carries me through my darkest days and helps me to remember the good times. He was my first-born child. I miss him so much that it takes my breath away. I will love and honor him forever.

In Memory of Capt. Joel E. Cahill
Killed when a roadside bomb detonated near his Humvee in Ad Dawr, Iraq
6/7/1971-11/6/2005

Home City and State: Papillion, NE
Military Branch/Unit: Company B, 1st Battalion, 15th Infantry Regiment, 3rd Brigade Combat Team, 3rd Infantry Division, U.S. Army
Dates Served: 1990-2005
Tour of Duty: Operation Iraqi Freedom
Locations Served: Fort Benning, GA; Iraq; Fort Bragg, NC

Biography
Joel graduated from Papillion-La Vista High School, Nebraska in 1989, and enlisted in the Army in early 1990. He thrived in his new environment. He hit the ground running, and never looked back. He became a life-long learner, taking advantage of every educational opportunity afforded him by the Army.

From a private in basic training to a captain and company commander, he served his country with honor and distinction during his 15-year career. His attitude and level of commitment may best be described by Lieutenant Colonel (LTC) Michael M. Kershaw, Battalion Commander, 1st Battalion, 75th Ranger Regiment, Hunter Army Airfield, GA: "Captain Cahill is a dynamic and aggressive officer whose performance stands above his peers in a battalion replete with hand-picked officers. The best of my four hand-picked Company Executive Officers, Joel is extremely intelligent, efficient and a master of his trade."

He took command of B Company, 1st Battalion, 15th Infantry Regiment in August 2005.

Captain Joel E. Cahill, 34, died in Ad Dawr, Iraq, on November 6, 2005, when an improvised explosive device detonated near his Humvee.

Achievements include:
- Ranger Tab
- Infantry Combat Badge
- Airborne Wings
- Air Assault Badge
- Jumpmaster
- Pathfinder
- Sapper Tab
- Ironman award
- Expert Infantryman's Badge
- General Douglas MacArthur Leadership Award (posthumous)

Medals include:
- Soldiers Medal
- Bronze Star
- Purple Heart
- Meritorious Service Medal
- Army Commendation Medal
- Army Achievement Medal
- National Defense Service Medal
- Global War on Terrorism Expeditionary Medal
- Global War on Terrorism Service Medal

Memories shared by Larry Cahill, Proud Father
President John F. Kennedy said, "The stories of past courage . . . can teach, they can offer hope, they can provide inspiration. But they cannot supply courage itself. For this, each man must look into his own soul."

Words do not adequately express my gratitude for the opportunity to share with you my son Joel's story of past courage. I offer this story to honor not only Joel, but all veterans, living and deceased, as well as our active duty servicemen and women. May their dedication to the military values of Loyalty, Duty, Respect, Selfless Service, Honor, Integrity and Personal Courage, serve as a guiding example to us all. I have selected the following three (of many), messages from memorial and guest book sites found on the Internet because of the brilliant color they add to any verbal portrait of my son Joel:

Today, as we remember the courage and sacrifices of our nation's soldiers, my mind wanders to Joel. I knew him in high school. I never knew the decorated soldier I read about. The Joel I knew was a smart-aleck teenager with a glint in his eye. He was a football player with an intensity, a restlessness, that clearly was his destiny in waiting. I never got to meet the man he grew into; but, when I read the stories about him, I'm overcome with pride.
Lynn (Painter) Kirkle, Omaha, Nebraska

"It seems like just yesterday, sir, you were giving me the green light to go ahead a shoot the moon to the apache flying above us. I was never more honored than the day you took over B Co.! From the moment you took over the company, I, as well as everyone, knew that you were a no nonsense kind of person. I would fight tooth and nail—to hell and back—if I knew you were the one leading me. I will see you on the flip side sir. CANNNNNNNNN DOOOOOO!"
James Foreman of San Juan, Puerto Rico

"I served under Captain Cahill when he was killed in Iraq. Never have I served under a finer commander than him. He truly loved his country and his command. Captain Cahill was loved by Baker Company, 1-15, 3rd ID, and he had our utmost respect. The impact he had on me will echo through the rest of my life. Thank you, sir, for everything."
Paul Ostby of Inver Grove Heights, MN

Captain Joel E. Cahill in the News

Articles featuring Captain Cahill were published in news outlets across the nation. These include "Soldier Says He's No Hero," from the Fayetteville Observer-Times, "GA Captain Remembered As a Committed Father" from the Washington Post by Staff Writer, Brigid Schulte, and "In Audie Murphy's Boots" from The Conservative Voice by Joseph Richard Gutheinz Jr.

We are grateful to all who have recounted Captain Cahill's service with such honor and dignity.

My Heroes

President Ronald Reagan said, "We have every right to dream heroic dreams. Those who say that we're in a time when there are no heroes, they just don't know where to look."

Joel, and his siblings, (Larry, Jr., Randall, Erin, and Jason), are all my heroes, and their lives honor my wife Barbara and me on a daily basis.

May I suggest that the next time we feel like complaining about how hard and long we've had to work, let us pause and reflect on the sacrifices both made, as well as the sacrifices that continue to be made every hour of every day around the world by all our servicemen and women. May I also suggest that the highest tribute we can pay to all who have gone before is to become the "best AMERICANs" we can be. Remember, every minute counts. Let us make it so in our lives. Let us remember that it's never enough to just show up. Let us strive to do our best in everything we do.

Joel, we will never forget.

We love you,
Mom and Dad

In Memory of Lance Cpl. Kyle Wain Codner
3/2/1985-5/26/2004
Died due to hostile action in Hit, Anbar Province, Iraq

Home City and State: Shelton, NE
Military Branch/Unit: 1st Combat Engineer Battalion, 1st Marine
Division, I Marine Expeditionary Force, U.S. Marine Corps
Dates Served: 6/16/2003-5/26/2004
Tour of Duty: Operation Iraqi Freedom
Locations Served: Iraq; Camp Pendleton, CA

Biography and Memories shared by Dixie Codner, Proud Mother:
Kyle grew up on a farm near Shelton, NE. He was a straight
A student and excelled at sports, especially basketball. He was
active in speech and drama, winning the state speech contest as a
freshman in high school with a humorous speech. Kyle was also
active in his church youth group, and participated in many mission
trips. Kyle was so moved by the events of 9/11 that he decided
he wanted to do something to make a difference in the world. He
thought he could do this by serving his country in the military. He
joined the United States Marine Corps right out of high school. He
graduated from boot camp with honors and quickly reached the
rank of Lance Corporal. In February of 2004, Kyle was deployed
to Iraq and was killed by an IED on May 26, 2004 at the age of
19. We had many great moments with Kyle from attending his
sporting events to just watching him grow up. He is greatly missed
by his parents Wain and Dixie Codner, his sister Melissa, and his
grandparents, aunts, uncles, cousins and many friends.

In Memory of Sgt. Aaron Brett Cruttenden
9/26/1985-11/7/2010
Died in Kunar Province, Afghanistan, of wounds suffered when
insurgents attacked his unit with small-arms fire

Home City and State: Norwood, CO
Military Branch/Unit: 161st Engineer Company, 27th Engineer
Battalion, 20th Engineer Brigade, U.S. Army

Dates Served: 3/16/2008-11/7/2010
Tour of Duty: Operation Enduring Freedom
Locations Served: Fort Leonard Wood, MO; Fort Bragg, NC; Kunar Province, Afghanistan

Biography:
Aaron was the first-born son and grandson and was the eldest of five children. He was born in Battle Creek, MI, and lived in Arkansas, Tennessee, Florida, Arizona and Colorado. He showed a love for the outdoors at an early age. He would often camp out and hike through the woods for days. Many of these adventures were his happiest times. He had a very diverse group of close friends and family, but he knew no strangers. He eventually settled into working as an electrical apprentice in Mesa, AZ during the winter months and as a tree trimmer during the summer months in Norwood, CO, which is where he called home.

His greatest and yet most fearful moment came when he found out he was to be a father. He felt a deep sense of being more responsible and stable to provide for his daughter. His answer to this was to join the Army. His pride in giving his all to whatever he did came through in his quick advancement in the Army and the great responsibility he felt for his brothers in arms.

His three brothers and one sister greatly looked up to him and consider him their hero. He was a thoughtful, giving and compassionate soul. He was wise beyond his mere 25 years. His main goal was to come home to his daughter. However, his duty to his fellow soldiers always came first. Thus, on November 7, 2010 when coming under fire, his first reaction was not of his own safety, but to get to his injured brothers.

Memories shared by Yvonne Featheringill, Proud Mother
Aaron was an amazing gift we were blessed to have in our lives. It is hard to narrow down a most memorable moment with our son—there are so many:

- The way he would always champion for the underdog, befriend the outcasts and stand up to the bullies.
- The pride he took in persevering to get his GED.
- Always caring for others before himself—especially when it came to looking out for his family.
- Even being deployed, his first question when calling home was always, "How's my baby girl?" His second was, "How's the family; is everyone doing ok?"

I think one of the best moments was when he brought his daughter home to meet the family for the first time. I'll always remember watching the pride and love in his eyes, mixed with the fear and vulnerability he felt at being responsible for this little person—his daughter. It was such a proud moment for us to watch him become a father—to see the way he stepped up to his responsibilities. Aaron was truly in awe of the privilege he felt for being able to be a dad. He loved his daughter dearly. Being able to be there and provide for her was his one and only goal in life from the moment he knew he was to be a dad.

In Memory of Lance Cpl. Leon B. Deraps
11/13/1986-5/6/2006
Killed while conducting combat operations against enemy forces in Anbar Province, Iraq

Home City and State: Jamestown, MO
Military Branch/Unit: 7th Engineer Support Battalion, 1st Marine Logistics Group, I Marine Expeditionary Force, U.S. Marine Corps
Tour of Duty: Operation Iraqi Freedom

Leon Deraps

Biography and Memories shared by Sandra Deraps, Proud Mother
Leon was born at the family's Jamestown, MO home on a bitter
cold morning, Nov. 13, 1986. The family called him their "Bonus
Baby," and he was strong with a sweet disposition. He answered to
Buddy, Bud, Uncle Lon, Bert and Bird Man.

He was protected and raised by his two older brothers who taught
him to take a punch and get up grinning; his three bossy sisters
who fought over the little guy too small to win an argument; his
veteran mom who believes in meals to set your clock by and who
taught him the patience to pick a row of green beans clean, and
to kneel at his bed and pray; his Marine Corps veteran father who
taught him how to hit the deck running, good to go, not to slouch
at flag ceremonies and how to sharpen his knife; and a community
best described as the "salt of the earth."

He grew up running in the soft hills and creek bottoms of the
Missouri River Valley. Always obedient, he was a good student,
anyone's friend and loved by all.

He went through Cub Scouts, Webelos, and earned rank quickly in the Boy Scouts. His achievements include 35 Merit Badges, the Order of the Arrow, a Rocky Mountain High Adventure Trek, National Boy Scout Jamboree 2001, Fort A.P. Hill, Virginia, a Philmont Scout Ranch Expedition 2002, Cimarron, New Mexico, all troop leadership positions, many service projects and Camporees. Under guidance from veteran Scouter Richard Schroeder, his Eagle project was the recovery of the abandoned Hardiman-Beatty AME Cemetery, just north of Jamestown. He was awarded the rank of Eagle Scout on March 13, 2005.

Leon participated in many sports at Moniteau C-1 School in Jamestown, including baseball, basketball, and track and field. He was also a member of the FFA, and he was voted prom king his senior year (2005). He also enjoyed many outdoor activities including hunting, fishing, and off-roading with his Jeep (when he wasn't pushing it). And, he was an active member of Annunciation Catholic Church, California, MO.

He was employed at Advanced Chimney Techniques of Jamestown, MO, and Cal's Thriftway, California, MO, before graduating high school. He pre-enlisted in the United States Marine Corps in the fall of 2004 while a senior in high school.

He graduated in May of 2005 and left for the Marine Corps Recruit Depot, San Diego, in June of 2005. Because of his Eagle Scout achievement, Leon entered the Marine Corps as a Private First Class. In September 2005, he graduated from Basic Training with many members of his proud family cheering him on.

He went on to complete Marine Combat Training at Camp Pendleton, California and Marine Corps Engineer School, Camp Lejeune, North Carolina. With his training completed in February 2006, he was deployed with members of his engineering unit to Fallujah, Iraq. Leon died during combat operations against enemy forces. However, "If the Army and the Navy ever look on Heaven's scenes, they will find the streets are guarded by United States Marines." He still stands his post—he's the one with the big grin, ear to ear.

Leon Deraps

In Memory of Cpl. Max W. Donahue
7/14/1987-8/7/2010
Died of wounds received while supporting combat operations in Helmand Province, Afghanistan

Home City and State: Highlands Ranch, CO
Military Branch/Unit: Marine Expeditionary Force Headquarters Group; Marine Expeditionary Force; U.S. Marines Corps
Tour of Duty: Operation Enduring Freedom

Biography and Memories shared by Julie Schrock, Proud Mother
The horror of September 11, 2001 did not end with the cleanup of Ground Zero. Horror seems too weak a word for families that have lost loved ones as a result of the attack. But I don't think a word has

been spoken or written that can adequately describe such a loss. So horror will have to suffice.

And, little did I know, the seed of my horror was planted on September 11, 2001. Max was 14 years old and in the eighth grade. I was a single mother to Max and his younger brother, Ryan, then 12 and in the sixth grade. It was several days after the attack on the twin towers when, while driving in our car, Max first told me of his intention to join the military. He said, "Mom, when I'm old enough I'm going to sign up to fight."

I replied, "Honey, as an American woman, that fills me with pride. But as your mother, it scares me to death."

Five years later, I dropped him off at the Marine recruiting station and hugged him goodbye as he left for Marine boot camp. I wondered, "How could this be happening? What took place that led up to this point? Why in the world did my first-born want to join the Marines?"

Now, I look back and try to piece together the puzzling answer to that question. Max was always very protective—always. There was a feeling of safety that came from just being around him. He took pride in his capacity to take care of people.

One day, after misjudging the amount of gas left in the tank, Max and Ryan were pushing their car into a gas station. As they stood in line to pay, they overheard the older man in front of the line discussing with the attendant the fact that the man's credit card was declined. The man was becoming frustrated. He didn't speak very good English and he didn't appear to have much money. Max plopped down the $55 that paid for the man's gas.

There was another time when my husband Chad, stepson Taylor, Max, Ryan and I were in the car. We passed a car that was stopped on the side of the road, obviously broken down. It was occupied by an elderly couple and their dog. I let the three boys out so they could push the car to a nearby gas station. (I can still envision Max blowing kisses to our cat as we drove away.) As I pulled into the gas station to pick up the boys, I watched as Max waved off the man's attempt to pay him.

I tell those stories in an attempt to draw a picture of the type of person Max was. But it's only half of Max's story. He was also a fighter. To quote one of his Marine buddies, "Max was a fighter, and a crazy one at that!" There was a trigger that seemed to go off in Max when fights broke out that took him to a "wild place." I would not have wanted to be on the other side of his flying fists. I think the combination of compassion and crazy is what made him such a good Marine.

These traits, coupled with an absolute fearlessness, are also what made him such a good working-dog handler. Max loved working with the dogs. His attitude was that no one was going to get the better of him, including the dogs he worked with. Max didn't take guff from people or from the dogs. He seems to share that characteristic with the other Marine dog handlers whom I've met.

And I've been privileged to meet some of the wonderful young Marines who served with Max. On one sunny Colorado Saturday, my family received a visit from eight of the Marines who were with Max in Afghanistan; two of whom were actually there after the IED exploded, taking Max's legs and his right arm. These precious, valiant Marines carried my son in whatever manner available to get him to the helicopter. I will forever be grateful for that visit. I told them that, although I live every day with the loss of my son, I don't have to shut my eyes and see it. I can't imagine the visions that never leave their views.

I was also able to tell them of the huge gift their visit had given to me. One of my heartbreaks was that Max was not with his family immediately after he suffered his wounds; that he wasn't with people who loved him or cared about him. I told this group of eight Marines that I now knew better; Max was absolutely surrounded by his brothers and I knew he was with people who loved and cared about him. What a gift to my heart that was and continues to be.

It's been almost one year since Max was wounded, died and buried. I spent many months of that first year writing the book, "Missing Max; Finding Hope After My Marine Son's Death." I wrote the book in an attempt to keep Max alive for as long as I could, and having a way that he could be remembered. I also wrote the book to try and understand how it was that I was able, and can continue, to live out my days. I'm different; but, I am not destroyed.

If I had to communicate just one message from the book, I would choose this one: If we had two minutes with a loved one who died—two minutes when we were not allowed to say anything and just listen to them—what would they say to us? What would Max say to me? What would I want him to say?

I'd want to hear, "Mom, I'm doing great up here. You won't believe how wonderful it is. Good job on the funeral. All is well with me. And Mom, thank you. Thank you for continuing to live and still be happy. Thank you for not letting this ruin your life. You didn't let me down and I'm proud of you. Watch out for Chad, Ryan and Taylor for me. See you soon."

It will be a long rest of my life without Max. But, I'll trade these years for eternity with him. Now, when I die, I want to hear well done from two people: Max and Jesus.

In Memory of Sgt. Joshua Andrew Ford
9/27/1985-7/31/2006
Killed during combat operations in Numaniyah, Iraq

Home City and State: Pender, NE
Military Branch/Unit: 189th Transportation Company, 485th Corps Support Battalion, Army National Guard
Dates Served: 2003-2006
Tour of Duty: Operation Iraqi Freedom
Honors: Bronze Star, Purple Heart, Combat Action Badge

Biography

Joshua Andrew Ford was born in Pender, Nebraska on September 27, 1985. He attended Wayne Public Schools until his junior year when he moved to Pender. Joshua enlisted in the Army National Guard his junior year. The summer after his high school graduation, Joshua attended boot camp at Fort Jackson, SC. He then attended AIT at Fort Leornard Wood, MO, where he learned to become a truck driver. Joshua attended Wayne State College the fall of 2004, where he hoped to major in art. Joshua's unit was deployed to Iraq in the fall of 2005; he was killed by an IED on July 31, 2006.

Memories shared by Lonnie Ford, Proud Father

While Joshua was home on leave at the end of April 2006, he told me something that will remain with me forever. Joshua looked at me and stated, "Old Man (his nickname for me), I now understand why you were so tough on me while I was growing up. You only wanted me to become the best person I could possibly be." My son had finally become a man and I was proud.

Chapter 2

G through R

Memoirs of fallen soldiers listed alphabetically by last name

In Memory of 1Lt. Kevin Gaspers
4/8/1981-4/23/2007
Killed when a makeshift bomb exploded near his location in Sadah, Iraq

Home City and State: Hastings, NE
Military Branch/Unit: 5th Squadron, 73rd Cavalry Regiment, 3rd
    Brigade Combat Team, 82nd Airborne Division, U.S. Army
Dates Served: 5/12/2005-4/23/2007
Tour of Duty: Operation Iraqi Freedom
Locations Served: Iraq

Biography
First Lieutenant Kevin Gaspers was born in Hastings, NE to John and Pam Gaspers. He graduated from St. Cecilia's High School in 2000, where he was an honor roll student. He was also a member of the football and wrestling teams. In 2005, he earned his bachelor's degree in accounting from the University of Nebraska at Lincoln. While at the University, he was Cadet Battalion Commander in the Army ROTC Program. He was a Scout Platoon Leader with the 5th Squadron, 73rd Cavalry Regiment, 3rd Brigade Combat Team, 82nd Airborne Division out of Ft. Bragg, North Carolina.

Memories shared by John and Pam Gaspers, Proud Parents
"Lt. Gaspers was a soft-spoken professional and a stellar officer," said Sgt. William Fleming. "Kevin was always checking up on the men and getting ready for the next mission. I don't think he ever slept. Kevin was one of 'the good ones.'"

We remember Kevin being home on leave March 22-April 8, 2007. Kevin took in activities that included his sister's track meet, visiting with his grandparents, getting together with friends and neighbors for supper, and sharing a special day with his older sister. Kevin was in correspondence with Alma's third grade class, and he went to visit them during his time home. They were very excited to see him and meet the soldier whom they had been writing.

We all have special memories of Kevin. He enjoyed the simple things in life. He loved John Wayne movies, the movie "Top Gun," country-western music, his friends, and his family.

In Memory of Spc. Russell Shane Hercules, Jr.
7/29/1987-10/1/2009
Died of wounds suffered when insurgents attacked his unit using small-arms fire in Wardak Province, Afghanistan

Home City and State: Murfreesboro, TN
Military Branch/Unit: Company F, 4th Battalion, 101st Aviation Regiment, 159th Combat Aviation Brigade, 101st Airborne Division, U.S. Army
Dates Served: 6/26/2006-10/1/2009
Tour of Duty: Operation Enduring Freedom
Locations Served: Fort Riley, KS; Fort Campbell, KY

Biography
Russell was 22 years old, born and raised in Murfreesboro, TN. He was a 2006 graduate of Blackman High School.

He always had a huge smile on his face and he knew how to make everyone around him smile. Always full of wisdom and helpful advice, He helped many through their rough times.

He completed tours in Iraq and Afghanistan. He got married and had his first son in June 2009. All he ever wanted was a family and he got that a few months prior to his death. He is survived by his wife Tori, son Christopher and stepdaughter Cadence. He is also survived by sister Jessica Hercules, nephew Joshua, mother Cheryl Tipton, stepfather Denver Tipton and father Russell Hercules, Sr.

Memories shared by Victoria Hercules, Proud Wife
I will always remember the day our son was born. Russell was still in Afghanistan, but he was on the phone with his mom who was in the delivery room. Through Skype, Russell was able to see his son for the first time, meet the doctors, and enjoy that first day with us.

I will never forget the first time Russell held our son, Christopher, in the airport on his R&R. These moments are forever instilled in my mind, and luckily we have pictures to show our son when he gets older.

In Memory of Pfc. Sam Williams Huff
7/12/1986-4/18/2005
Died of injuries sustained on April 17 in a makeshift bomb attack

Home City and State: Tucson, AZ
Military Branch/Unit: 170th Military Police Company, 504th Military Police Battalion, 42nd Military Police Brigade, U.S. Army
Dates Served: 6/1/2004-4/18/2005
Tour of Duty: Operation Iraqi Freedom
Locations Served: Fort Leonard Wood, MO; Fort Lewis, WA; Baghdad, Iraq

Biography and Memories shared by Jane Knight, Proud Grandmother
Sam was born July 12, 1986, on her dad's birthday. She was known as "Sweet Pea" to her daddy and "Peaches" to her mom.

From a very early age, she had a personality that completely stole your heart. She was bright far beyond her years. And, she was a born negotiator who knew how to engineer "win-win" situations, even at an early age. She knew how to encourage others to see her point of view and make everyone happy in the end. She carried this gift with her all through her school years and into the military. Sam "championed the underdog" and extended a compassionate hand and heart to those less fortunate than herself.

Although Sam has been described by many as a "girly girl," her seargent, Sam James, said it best when he stated, "Sam had no fear. She had a backbone of steel even though she was barely five foot tall and weighed 100 lbs."

She was a soldier's soldier, and she was determined to succeed as a soldier. This was not surprising since she had excelled at nearly everything she had tackled since childhood. She had a "can do" attitude that shone so brightly she drew the attention of those in authority wherever she went.

There has been a book written about Sam called, "American Daughter: The Sam Huff Story," by Leslie Ann Garrison. It tells the story of a very remarkable, special human being. Her time on this earth was way too brief. This world is a much better place because Pfc. Sam W. Huff was a part of it.

Every moment I got to spend with Sam was a "special, favorite moment."

To all of us whose lives you've touched and of us become a part,
You've left these little footprints of Love upon our hearts.
We'll know that you are there with every setting sun
And we'll love you forever until our time on earth is done.
I love you
"Grammie Jane"

In Memory of Sgt. Issac Brandon Jackson
4/2/1982-10/27/2009
Died in Arghandab Valley, Afghanistan, of wounds suffered when enemy forces attacked his vehicle with a makeshift bomb

Home City and State: Plattsburg, MO
Military Branch/Unit: 1st Battalion, 17th Infantry Regiment, 5th Stryker Brigade Combat Team, 2nd Infantry Division, U.S. Army
Dates Served: 5/24/2004-10/27/2009
Tour of Duty: Operation Enduring Freedom
Locations Served: Fort Drum, NY; Fort Lewis, WA; Afghanistan

Biography

Issac was born in St. Joseph, MO. His father John E. Jackson died when he was just 14 months old. Issac lived with his mother Christal and his brothers Larry and Jeremy Jackson.

He attended school in Plattsburg. He graduated in 2001 from Lathrop High School in Lathrop, MO, where he participated in wrestling, football and basketball. He was also a member of the FHA.

He joined the First Baptist Church in Lathrop, where he was an active member. At church, he met and later married his wife Kristen.

He joined the Army on May 24, 2004. After completing basic training at Fort Benning, GA, he was stationed at Fort Drum, NY, in 132 Infantry Battalion, 3rd Brigade, 10th Mountain Division. He was stationed there when he deployed for the first time to Afghanistan in March 2006. This deployment came to an end in June 2007, after which Issac and Kristen transferred to Fort Lewis, WA. Their son, Enoch, was born while he was stationed in Fort Lewis.

He deployed to Afghanistan for the second time in May 2009. Issac and Kristen found out they were going to have another baby—this time a girl. They were so excited.

He was killed in Arghandab Valley in the Kandahar Province, Afghanistan, when his Stryker unit was struck by an IED buried in the river bed, killing Issac and six other men. Kristen gave birth to their daughter, Eden, 47 days after Issac was killed in action. He was a good and loving son, brother, husband and father. He will be forever loved and missed by all of us.

Memories shared by Christal A. Thomas-Karker, Proud Mother
My favorite moment with my son was watching him with his son. He loved his son and was so excited about the baby girl arriving. There are so many things I remember while he was growing up.

Every time he saw me, he would hug me and kiss my cheek. When we talked he always said, "Momma, I love you." These are words I will never hear from him again.

In Memory of Pfc. John Corey Johnson
6/30/1982-5/27/2011
Died of wounds suffered when insurgents attacked his Mine-Resistant Ambush-Protected vehicle with recoilless rifle fire and rocket-propelled grenades as it traveled in a convoy in the Nalgham area of Kandahar Province, Afghanistan

Home City and State: Prescott, AZ
Military Branch/Unit: 1st Battalion, 32nd Infantry Regiment, 3rd
    Brigade Combat Team, 10th Mountain Division, U.S. Army
Dates Served: 2/23/2010-5/27/2011
Tour of Duty: Operation Enduring Freedom
Locations Served: Afghanistan

Biography and Memories shared by Jennifer Rose Johnson, Proud Wife
We never called John by his first name. He was known as Corey. Corey was a great man, a true friend, the best husband I could ever ask for, and an exceptional father of our beautiful little girls—Marina McKena and Rae LeAnn Corey (he was never able to meet her).

Corey was one of the most enjoyable people to be around. He had a great sense of humor and he could always bring laughter to a room—no matter how bad things were.

All in all, Corey was a happy man. He loved playing jokes on people and enjoyed hunting and fishing. Corey also loved spending time with his family, whether it was playing Xbox with his oldest daughter or bringing her to the "Build-A-Bear" workshop.

Corey's family was his everything, and I am so proud to be able to call him my husband. He was the man who would give the shirt off his back to help others, even if he knew he couldn't afford it.

Corey, you are greatly missed. My best moment with my husband would have to be when we were on our way to the mall with our daughter, Marina, when she says, "Daddy, can you please put in Lady Gaga?" Corey turned on the music and started dancing and singing the "Poker Face" song. I couldn't stop laughing.

One other time I will keep in my heart forever was March 16, 2011-the last night I ever spent with my husband because on March 17, 2011, Corey deployed. We spent the night with our five-year-old daughter, Marina, watching Charlie and the Chocolate Factory.

Corey and I were married on February, 15, 2011-one month before he deployed. He left me with the best gift in the world—he blessed me with one more beautiful little girl, Rae LeAnn Corey. I will always have my husband with me.

In Memory of Sgt. Jonathan M. Keller
5/15/1979-1/24/2009
Died following complications of a gunshot wound suffered on the Pakistan border

Home City and State: Wading River, NY
Military Branch/Unit: New York National Guard, C Troop, 2nd Squadron, 101st Calvary, U.S. Army Reserves
Dates Served: 6/16/2005-1/24/2009
Tours of Duty: Operation Iraqi Freedom, Operation Enduring Freedom
Locations Served: Forward Operating Base Fortress, NAWA Pass; Nalay Observation Post, Khas Konar, Binshai Pass; Forward Operating Base, Sarkani, Camp Joyce

Special Military Honors
Purple Heart, Army Commendation Medal, Meritorious Service Medal, Combat Infantry Badge, New York State Conspicuous

Service Cross, Army Reserve Component Achievement Medal, Afghanistan Campaign Medal with Silver Service Star, Armed Forces Reserve Medal, Armed Forces Expeditionary Medal, NATO Medal, Global War on Terrorism Service Medal

Biography
Jonathan Keller was born May 15, 1979, in Wading River, NY. One of four children, he was the second child and eldest son. He was particularly close to his two younger brothers, Joshua and Michael, and served as their confidante, coach, and cheerleader throughout grade school and college.

He joined the U.S. Navy after high school. He served on the nuclear carrier USS John Stennis during Operation Iraqi Freedom. After service, he decided to concentrate on completing college and focus on becoming a certified personal trainer. A life-long passion for personal fitness and a strong discipline in good health led him to this career. He earned a certificate in physical training from Hofstra University and pursued an undergraduate degree in health sciences. He really enjoyed his work as a personal trainer and developed a following of dedicated clients.

While taking college courses, Jonathan joined the New York State Army Reserve, 1st Battalion, the famous Fighting 69th. A proud American, he would say, "If not me, then who will fight for our country, its values, and its freedoms?"

In late 2007, his unit was called to serve in Afghanistan during Operation Enduring Freedom. He was shipped to Kabul in early 2008 and assigned to the 172nd Airborne Brigade, Camp Joyce, in the deadly Kunar Provence.

After numerous border ambushes, he sustained critical gunshot wounds during one engagement. His injury and heroism earned him the Purple Heart, Army Commendation Medal, and the Meritorious Medal. He died suddenly in January 2009 after enduring numerous operations in an Army hospital, and was posthumously promoted to the rank of Sergeant.

He had a contagious smile and a passionate, generous heart. His family is proud of his selfless acts of courage.

Memories shared by Martin Keller, Proud Father

Jonathan had a passion for physical fitness and that passion led him into the demanding sport of wrestling. With an early start in middle school through high school, he trained and practiced with improved skills. He endured many setbacks but never entertained the thought of resigning from this sport, for he loved the competitiveness and team spirit.

During his high school years, he and his younger brother were in the same weight bracket and, all too often, he would be forced to wrestle off with his younger brother to decide who would wrestle in team competition. Jonathan decided to step aside and conceded the weight bracket to his brother and awaited a future opportunity when this weight differential was no longer consequential to either brother.

On a significant team meet, Jonathan had been given the opportunity by his coach to wrestle a highly regarded and highly ranked opponent. An extremely competitive match, his endurance proved to be the deciding factor and he defeated this opponent by pinning him in the waning moments of the third and final period.

As parents, we were so proud of his accomplishments. For all of his hard work and focus in this sport he had achieved such a proud moment. This was truly a defining victory for Jonathan and for his team. This moment revealed Jonathan's moral fiber and showed hard work, focus and perseverance can overcome life's obstacles, traits he carried into the service of his country.

In Memory of Cpl. Brandon Michael Kirton

10/01/1985-05/18/2011

Died of wounds suffered when insurgents attacked his unit with small-arms fire and mortar rounds in Bur-Mohammad, Kandahar Province, Afghanistan

Home City and State: Englewood, CO
Military Branch/Unit: 2nd Battalion, 502nd Infantry Regiment, 2nd Brigade Combat Team, 101st Airborne Division, U.S. Army
Dates Served: 01/2008-05/18/2011
Tour of Duty: Operation Enduring Freedom
Locations Served: Afghanistan, Iraq

Special Military Honors

Bronze Star, Purple Heart, Distinguished Member of the 502nd Regiment, Army Commendation Medal, Army Achievement Medal, Good Conduct Medal, National Defense Service Medal, Afghan and Iraq Campaign Medals, Global War on Terrorism Service Medal, Army Service Ribbon, Overseas Service Ribbon, North Atlantic Treaty Organization Medal, Combat Infantryman Badge

Biography

Brandon was born October 1, 1985, to Kathy and Bob Kirton in Englewood, Colorado. He grew up in the house his dad grew up in and attended the same schools as his dad. He attended Cherrelyn Elementary School, Flood Middle School and graduated from Englewood High School in May 2006.

He loved to play sports. He started playing baseball, soccer and basketball at the age of five. He lettered in baseball and soccer in high school.

He was full of energy and forever on the go. He was adventurous and had no fear. He loved a challenge and was never afraid to try new experiences like skydiving in Hawaii or swimming with sharks.

At an early age, Brandon expressed his desire to become a soldier. He fulfilled that dream by joining the Army in January 2008. He took great pride in serving his country and was a dedicated soldier.

He also had a great desire to have a family of his own. On July 29, 2010, Brandon became a father. His daughter, Heaven, was born while he was deployed in Afghanistan. Although he was not able to be home in time for her birth, he did get to see Heaven when she was seven weeks old. He spent two weeks with her before returning to Afghanistan. He was twelve days from completing his tour when he was killed in Kandahar by small arms fire on May 18, 2011.

Brandon is survived by his daughter Heaven; his parents Bob and Kathy Kirton; his sisters Brittney, Tiffany and Stephanie; his brother-in-law Mike, and his niece Lorelei.

Memories shared by Kathy Kirton, Proud Mother
In May 2010, our family traveled to California so we could spend time with Brandon before he deployed to Afghanistan in June. California was one of our favorite places to vacation as we had been there many times as a family over the years. We went to watch Brandon's favorite baseball team, the Colorado Rockies, play the LA Dodgers and San Diego Padres. We experienced the Hollywood Walk of Fame for the first time, visited Venice Beach, Runyon State Park, explored downtown San Diego, hung out at Malibu Beach and ate at some great restaurants. We reminisced about vacations we had taken and all the great times we spent together. We laughed a lot, took hundreds of pictures and just enjoyed each other's company.

Brandon was expecting his first child in July and we talked a lot about her. He was so excited about becoming a father and shared with us all his hopes and dreams for his baby girl, Heaven. We were so happy to see Brandon beam with such pride and joy over becoming a daddy!

We also took time to reflect on Brandon's deployment. We told him how proud we were of him, how we would miss him immensely and that we would pray for his, and all of the soldiers', safe return home.

We were so grateful to have had this time with Brandon. The memories we shared on this last trip with him as a family will be forever in our hearts. We love you, Brandon.

In Memory of Sgt. Bradley Wayne Marshall
8/28/1969-7/31/2007
Killed by enemy indirect fire in Tunis

Home City and State: Little Rock, AR
Military Branch/Unit: Battery B, 2nd Battalion, 377th Field
Artillery Regiment, 4th Brigade Combat Team, 25th Infantry
Division, U.S. Army
Dates Served: 1/20/2006-7/31/2007
Tour of Duty: Operation Iraqi Freedom
Locations Served: Fort Benning, GA; Fort Richardson, AK; Iraq

Biography
Brad was a very good athlete that people seemed to look up to. He never said a bad word about anyone.

He first joined the Army in 1990. He was in the Army for four years. After that, he remained in the Army Reserves for another four years. Then, he and his dad ran a very successful construction company together. He had married by this time and had two sons. He built a beautiful home close to his parents and seemed to be very happy.

When 9/11 happened, Brad started talking about going back into the military. Of course, his parents tried to talk him out of it; he said he just couldn't stand by while his fellow soldiers died for our country. He got busy working out and convincing his wife and children that he really needed to do this. So, in 2006 he went back into the military.

With his family's blessing, he sold his home and moved his family to Fort Richardson, AK. From there, he was sent to Iraq. He was so proud to be a forward observer and FiSTer with the US Army. He was a lot older than most of the guys, many of whom have become friends of the family. They tell his parents how they looked up to Brad. He loved God, his family and country.

Memories shared by Fran Marshall, Proud Mother

Brad played football and baseball, and he was very good at both. I remember, I told one of my co-workers that Brad would take her daughter (who attended another school) to the prom. Of course, he had a high school game and it went into overtime. He didn't want to leave the game early so I went and got his tux and brought it to the baseball field so he could get ready there.

We heard from so many people after Brad's death—even the real estate person told us how Brad looked and looked for the perfect house to move his family to in Alaska, and how she visited them after they had moved in. His wife made the house into a real home. After Brad was killed, the packers wrote us and talked about how touching it was to pack the pictures, bibles, and all the things that make a home.

In Memory of Lance Cpl. Christopher Steele Meis
2/1/1991-3/17/2011
Died while conducting combat operations in Helmand Province, Afghanistan.

Home City and State: Bennett, CO
Military Branch/Unit: 2nd Battalion, 8th Marine Regiment, 2nd Marine Division, II Marine Expeditionary Force, U.S. Marines Corps
Dates Served: 1/11/2010-3/17/2011
Tour of Duty: Operation Enduring Freedom
Locations Served: Camp Lejeune, NC; Helmand Province, Afghanistan

Biography
Although born Christopher Steele Meis, his family never called him Christopher. They always called him Steele. He was affectionately known to all of his family as Steele-Man.

Steele knew from early on he wanted to be in the military and had it dialed down to the Marines by eighth grade. He was an avid hunter and outdoorsman.

School was not necessarily his thing. Well, the academia aspect of school was not his thing. But, he was all over the social aspect of school. His mother believes he charmed his way through high school.

He had high expectations of the people in his life; but, he was willing to give his all in return. He was a true friend. He enjoyed laughing, and he didn't take life too seriously. He was all about family and the Marines.

Memories Shared by Holly Meis, Proud Mother
Although we had no intention of our son being called anything other than Steele, with an unusual last name—Meis (pronounced Mice)—I thought we had better give him something more normal to fall back on. So we gave him his Father's name—Christopher—and made Steele his middle name. When he arrived, the nickname Steele-Man stuck.

One day when Steele was in the third grade, he came home from school and said, "Mom, can you call me John?" When I asked him why, he said, "I just like John." I explained that we couldn't and wouldn't call him John. I told him he had one of the coolest names around and that one day he was going to thank me for giving him that name, especially when girls came into the picture. He was upset but went on with his day. Then, one day when he was a sophomore in high school, Steele came home from school, kissed me hello and walked to his room. Halfway there he stopped and said, "Oh, mom, thank you for naming me Steele." I just smiled and said, "You're welcome, baby." There was no further discussion, but I knew . . . and I just smiled.

I am Steele's Grandma-ma. Steele was my daughter's first born. He was a delightful child—full of energy and a little mischievous. He soon became the "apple of my eye," and we were buddies almost from the start. As Steele got older, he would spend weekends with my husband and me. Steele and I would talk for hours. We also spent a lot of time in Toys R Us! He loved guns and probably owned at least one of every toy gun made. One of my favorite memories of Steele-Man was an incident when he was about eight or nine years old. He and his mother were visiting one day. As they were leaving, I grabbed my trash and walked out with them. We said our good-byes, they drove off and I walked through the side gate to put my trash in the trash can. When I turned around, there stood Steele-Man. He threw his arms around me and said, "I love you Grandma-ma," and ran back to the car. He got in and they drove off again. I called his mom to ask what that was all about, and she said that as they drove off Steele said, "I love that woman." So his mom said, "Then, you should tell her that." She backed up; he jumped out and ran up and said that to me. My heart melted. It was one of the sweetest moments of my lifetime. As Steele-Man got older and started to drive, he would come to see me often. He would ring the doorbell and hide so when I opened the door it appeared no one was there. Then, he would step out, grinning from ear to ear. He was such a delight and I love him more than words can describe. I am so proud of him and miss him terribly! *Christine Arnold, Proud Grandmother*

I am Steele's aunt. My husband, Bob, and I are his godparents. Steele was a typical boy. When Steele was about 8 years old, we were watching him and his brother, Hunter, at our home. Every time a woman came on the TV with a low cut blouse or something, Steele would start hooting and hollering. We had to keep changing the channel and, finally, had to watch a cartoon. I remember his Uncle Bob and I laughed so hard when that happened. Steele grew up to be a wonderful man. He was always very respectful. That guy loved anything to do with the outdoors and we spent wonderful times camping and fishing. We also had many talks together during his lifetime—we were very close. Of course, Steele was a "guy's guy," so he spent most of his time with his Uncle Bob and the men. I am very grateful for the time I was able to spend with him, and I think about him every day.

After Steele's passing, we went up to his favorite camping spot to celebrate his life and spread his ashes. During that evening, on a spot we called Coyote Hill, as we talked about our experiences with Steele, the clouds over us formed into the shape of an Eagle with its wings raised just like the symbol of United State Marine Corps. It was the most peaceful and inspirational moment I have ever experienced in my life.

Sheryl Guerra, Proud Aunt and Godparent

I am Steele's uncle. My wife, Sheryl, and I are his godparents. Family was everything to Steele. The summer before Steele enlisted in the Marine Corps, we had a BBQ out at our ranch in Eastern Colorado. We had the shotguns out and shot skeet for hours. Steele was a great shot. When it came time to eat, Steele helped me BBQ. We cooked some bear meat and Steele was walking around eating it right off the end of a big hunting knife. One of the neighbors who had too much to drink was getting obnoxious and, as I went to talk to the neighbor, I leaned over to Steele and said, "You have my back?" Steele said, "Hell yeah, I have your back, Uncle Bob." It was great! Also, when Steele was about 8 or 9 years old, we went camping at Eleven Mile Reservoir. We were fishing when Steele asked me, "Uncle Bob, what type of bait are you using?" I told him and asked him if he wanted to try it; then I helped him bait his pole. A few minutes passed and I saw a big fish jump out of the water. About the same time, Steele yelled, "Uncle Bob, I got a fish!" His father, Chris, and I ran to see. We watched Steele pull in a two-and-a-half pound rainbow trout. You should have seen the look on his face—he had a smile from ear to ear. He was definitely the fisherman of the trip. Needless to say, we had fish that night.

Bob Guerra, Proud Uncle and Godparent

My name is Casandra Salberg, one of Steele's high school teachers. As a teacher, I have had the pleasure of getting to know many wonderful young people. But, every now and then I get a student who makes me work—Steele was one of those students as school was more of a social endeavor for him, but if he happened to learn something while he was in school, that was ok too. The first day I had Steele as a student was in American Government during his junior year. After reviewing my expectations of the kids and explaining how things would work that semester, Steele was leaving for his next class . . . as he reached the door, he looked

back and said, "You should meet my mom; you sound just like her."
As the years passed, his mom Holly and I did become friends. I
was privileged to watch Steele grow into a wonderful man through
her eyes. Steele was home for Christmas. Then, in January before
he left for Afghanistan, he came by the school to say, "Hi." The
laid-back boy I taught in school stood before me a proud Marine.
We talked for a while; the entire time I was thinking how proud
and happy I was that he had pursued his dream and that it was
everything he hoped it would be. As he was leaving, I told him to
be careful and keep in touch when he could. He turned and smiled
"that smile" and said, "It's all good Mrs. S."
Casandra Salberg, Proud High School Teacher

In Memory of Staff Sgt. Robert James Miller
10/14/1983-1/25/2008
Killed when he encountered small arms fire while conducting
combat operations in Barikowt, Afghanistan

Home City and State: Oviedo, FL
Military Branch/Unit: Operational Detachment Alpha 3312,
    Company A, 3rd Battalion, 3rd Special Forces Group, U.S. Army
Dates Served: 2003-2008
Tour of Duty: Operation Enduring Freedom
Special Military Honors: Medal of Honor, 2010; Purple
    Heart; Bronze Star; Meritorious Service Medal; two Army
    Commendation Medals with Valor Device

Rob Miller

Biography

Born in Pennsylvania, Robert James Miller grew up in the Chicago suburb of Wheaton, Illinois. Rob displayed a natural athletic ability at an early age, and was always interested in history and military affairs. He developed a passion for gymnastics in high school, spending hours in the gym every day and leading his team to the state tournament his senior year. He demonstrated an aptitude for foreign languages, studying German and Latin in high school, and French and Pashto while in the Army.

The 2001 terrorist attacks made a deep impression on Rob, and he signed his enlistment papers 15 months later. He soon began rigorous Special Forces training, received his Green Beret in March 2005, and was assigned to Third Special Forces Group as a Weapons Sergeant. Rob first deployed to Afghanistan in August 2006, where he earned two Army Commendation Medals with

Valor Device for courage against enemy forces. He then attended Ranger school before redeploying to Afghanistan in October 2007.

In the early morning of January 25, 2008, Rob, his Special Forces team, and a partnered Afghan National Army unit, were ambushed in mountainous eastern Afghanistan. He remained at the front of the patrol, laying down withering suppressive fire, calling out locations of the insurgents to the rest of the patrol, and directing the ANA soldiers. After his captain was critically wounded, Rob advanced on the insurgents, drawing fire on himself, allowing the rest of the patrol to reach cover. Even after being shot, he continued the fight until no longer able to do so. He was posthumously awarded the nation's highest award for valor, the Medal of Honor, on October 6, 2010.

Memories shared by Phillip and Maureen Miller, Proud Parents
Midway through his two years of Special Forces training, Rob called from Fort Bragg: he would be coming down to Florida to visit for the weekend. Surf was up, and that was likely the main reason he was coming. When told a hurricane might be on the way, he replied, "So?"

Hurricane Charley's impact was much worse than expected. While the rest of the family was hunkered down with the doors and windows shaking, Rob spent most of that wild evening enjoying the show, looking out our big, glass double front doors. He was upset when we insisted that no one go out. Of course, when the adults were out of the room, he did go out. He danced in the wind and rain in front of his younger siblings yelling, "Look at me, I'm in a hurricane!"

Our neighborhood had a fair amount of property damage. The immediate problem was the large number of fallen trees, many of which prevented access to homes. The next morning Rob, without any hesitation, was out clearing logs and brush. He remarked a number of people had been standing around surveying damage and he felt someone should lead by example and just start working. Within minutes, a number of others picked up and got the necessary work done. After that, it was off to the beach! That weekend demonstrated Rob's personality well—his fearless sense of adventure, his willingness to lend a helping hand, and his love of the outdoors.

In Memory of Spc. Matthew Michael Murchison
10/11/1985-8/4/2007
Killed when the vehicle he was in was struck by a roadside bomb in Baghdad, Iraq

Home City and State: Independence, MO
Military Branch/Unit: 127th Military Police Company, 720th Military Police Battalion, 89th Military Police Brigade, U.S. Army
Dates Served: 9/25/2005-8/4/2007
Tour of Duty: Operation Iraqi Freedom
Locations Served: Fort Leonard Wood, MO; Hanau, Germany; FOB Kalsu, Iraq

Biography:
Spc. Matthew M. Murchison was killed on August 4, 2007, in Baghdad, Iraq, by an attack on his vehicle by an improvised explosive device. He was assigned to the 127th MP Company, 720th MP Battalion, 89th MP Brigade. He is survived by parents Michael Murchison and Debbie Murchison-Perri, sister Melissa Murchison, aunts, uncles, cousins and many dear friends. He will be missed.

Memories shared by Debbie Murshison-Perri, Proud Mother
Matthew always wanted to be a police officer—like his father—when he was young. He did not want to go to college, but rather to serve his country and get the training he would need to obtain his dream of being like his dad. He had hopes of being an Olathe, Kansas police officer. He got to do what he loved the most. We, his family, are so very proud of what he accomplished.

Until we meet, again, sweet son.

In Memory of Pfc. Andrew Henning Nelson
3/31/1987-12/25/2006
Killed when a makeshift bomb detonated near his vehicle during
combat operations in Baghdad, Iraq

Home City and State: St. Johns, MI
Military Branch/Unit: Company A, 9th Engineer Battalion, 2nd
  Brigade Combat Team, 1st Infantry Division, U.S. Army
Dates Served: 7/12/2005-12/25/2006
Tour of Duty: Operation Iraqi Freedom
Locations Served: Schweinfurt, Germany; Baghdad, Iraq

Biography
Andrew was the kind of person who wanted to serve others. When
he was about 3 years old, when the garbage truck would come
he would say, "I want to be a garbage man when I grow up." He
quickly graduated from garbage man to a fireman. The family
couldn't drive past a fire hall without checking out the fire trucks.
Then he wanted to become a policeman. His grandmother made
him an authentic looking police uniform, which he proudly wore
everywhere. By the time he was about 10, he had started playing
Army. He would constantly pretend he was a soldier and sneak up
on people and pretend to shoot the enemy.

Andrew was about 14 years old when 9/11 happened. From that
moment on, his family knew he would become a soldier. He
was old enough to understand what had happened and he took it
personally, like any proud American would. He entered the Army
in the Delayed Entry Program, and started doing some training on
nights and weekends during his senior year of high school.

He graduated from high school in June of 2005 and left for Basic/
AIT Training on July 12, 2005. He graduated from Basic/AIT
at the end of October 2005, and then married his high school
sweetheart, Kristi, on November 5, 2005. At the end of November,
he left for Germany. He deployed to Kuwait on September 1, 2006,
and then onto Baghdad in mid-October 2006. On Christmas Day

2006, Andrew was killed instantly when an IED detonated near his vehicle. He died living his dream.

He is survived by his parents Alan and Tami Nelson and sisters Jessica and Stephanie.

Memories shared by Alan Nelson, Proud Father
We had a lot of favorite moments with Andrew. Andrew was our first child. He was my first, and only, son. I couldn't have been more proud. Andrew was well liked by everybody. He was a smart kid with a lot going for him. He could have done anything he wanted. When Andrew graduated from high school he took the $2,000 he got for graduation and put it into a Roth IRA. He did that all on his own. I was very proud of him; a lot of kids would have just blown the money, but he invested it.

Andrew was also a great swimmer, and we have a lot of great memories from his competitive swimming. Andrew started swimming competitively when he was about 9 years old and continued through high school. He was a four-year varsity letter winner and was team captain his senior year. Andrew was very competitive—he didn't like to get beat. So, many times he would be a body length or so behind someone, but would really turn it on and win the race. He usually swam the butterfly and the individual medley.

When Andrew was little, we played Legos all the time. He had such a great imagination; we would build all kinds of things. We continued to play Legos right up to the night before he left for the Army. And, we would still pull out the Legos once in a while if we were bored. When Andrew got to Germany, he called and wanted us to send him the Legos. So, we did; he and all of his Army buddies played Legos before they deployed. We had a lot of great memories playing Legos.

In Memory of Sgt. Nicholas Santo Nolte
9/16/1979-11/24/2004
Died at the National Naval Medical Center in Bethesda, MD, from injuries sustained on Nov. 8 in a roadside bomb blast in Baghdad

Home City and State: Falls City, NE
Military Branch/Unit: 2nd Low Altitude Air Defense Battalion, 2nd Marine Aircraft Wing, 2nd Marine Expeditionary Force, Marine Corps Air Station, U.S. Marine Corps
Dates Served: 1998-2002, reenlisted 2003-2004
Tour of Duty: Operation Iraqi Freedom
Special Military Honors: Purple Heart, Joint Service Achievement Medal, Presidential Service Badge

Biography
Sgt. Nicholas Santo Nolte, 25, died at National Navy Medical Center at Bethesda, Maryland. He was born Sept. 16, 1979, to Anita (Santo) and the late Bradley Nolte. He was raised in Falls City and graduated from Falls City Sacred Heart School in 1998. He was a member of Sts. Peter and Paul Catholic Church in Falls City. Following graduation, he joined the United States Marine Corps. He served in HMX-1 (First Marine Helicopter Squadron) providing security for President Clinton and President Bush. He married Melina Pepe on Febuary 27, 2001, in Quantico, VA. After serving four years, Nicholas moved to Keene, NY with his wife and their daughter Alanna.

He then re-enlisted on February 27, 2003, and began recruiting duty in Plattsburgh, NY. He attended Low Altitude Air Defense School at Fort Bliss, TX. After graduating from there, he was stationed at Cherry Point Marine Air Station, NC. He deployed to Iraq with the 24th Marine Expeditionary Unit aboard the USS Kearsarge on June 9, 2004. On Nov. 9, while serving in Al Anbar Province, Iraq, he was providing security for a colonel when the Humvee he and five others were traveling in was hit by a roadside bomb. He sustained multiple injuries as a result of that enemy action. He was transferred to Landstuhl, Germany, and then Bethesda, Maryland, where he died on Nov. 24, 2004.

Memories shared by Melina Nolte, Proud Wife

Nicholas is described by his mother as being "a pure joy to raise; he was a happy loving little boy" who gave her so many wonderful memories. Nick is remembered by her as being always happy and loving with a great enthusiasm for life. Her favorite memories include exploring in the timbers, four wheeler rides, planting the garden and farm chores. Just watching the storm roll in together or going for a ride in his truck were special times for them.

When Nicholas was 3 years old, he came down on Christmas morning to find a three-wheeler waiting for him. Always enthusiastic, he was so excited he got right on it and drove it up the wall! Nicholas always did everything to the fullest.

He also was very determined, a trait that served him well in the Marine Corps. Once, Nicholas had to get a cow to let him lead her for the 4-H fair. The cow was very stubborn and would have none of it. So one day Nicholas' parents discovered him in a white tank top and blue jeans, driving a tractor with a rope tied to it with the cow at the end of it! He never was the kind to give up.

In Memory of Lance Cpl. Rex Arthur Page, Sr.
12/24/1984-6/28/2006
Died from wounds received during combat operations in Taqaddum, Anbar Province, Iraq

Home City and State: Kirksville, MO
Military Branch/Unit: 3rd Battalion, 5th Marine Regiment, 1st Marine Division, I Marine Expeditionary Force, U.S. Marine Corps
Dates Served: 5/5/2005-6/28/2006
Tour of Duty: Operation Iraqi Freedom
Locations Served: 29 Palms, CA; Fallujah, Iraq

Biography and Memories shared by Larry Page, Proud Father
Rex was born and raised in Kirksville, MO. He possessed a strong faith in God and had a close relationship with his parents and his younger brother, James.

He loved people and he loved serving with his Marine brothers. Since the third grade, he wanted to become a Marine. When he graduated Kirksville Christian High, he entered Marine Corps. We will forever remember and cherish his phone calls home. He was always upbeat. He would joke about him being a Marine and his dad being a sailor. One of my favorite moments was when I called him a Marine for the first time.

In Memory of Sgt. Adam James Ray
3/9/1986-2/9/2010
Died of wounds suffered when insurgents attacked his unit with a roadside bomb near Camp Bastion in Helmand Province, Afghanistan

Home City and State: Louisville, KY
Military Branch/Unit: 4th Battalion, 23rd Infantry Regiment, 5th
　　Stryker Brigade Combat Team, 2nd Infantry Division, U.S. Army
Dates Served: 6/10/2005-3/9/2010
Tour of Duty: Operation Enduring Freedom
Locations Served: Fort Benning, GA; Camp Casey, Korea; Fort
　　Lewis, WA; Southern Afghanistan

Biography and Memories shared by Donna Ray, Proud Mother
In the third grade, Adam visited an Army museum, and ever since, he wanted to become a soldier. Adam researched everything he could about the Army. In the fifth grade, he created a small-scale World War I dramatization of the trench warfare, which was placed on display in a public library.

When Adam was in the eleventh grade, he turned 18 years old and joined the Army. That summer he went to Basic Training. But, at the end of his training, Adam had to return to complete his senior year in high school. Because he fell ill, Adam was not able to complete his training and had to repeat his Basic Training the following summer. While most people would be discouraged, Adam loved going back. He went with the attitude that he can help the others because he knew what was expected. And, that's exactly what he did. In fact, Adam graduated with honors from Basic and AIT.

Adam was displaced in the wrong Military Occupational Specialty. To become Infantry, he had to reenlist. So, again, that's exactly what he did. He went from a Hospital Medical Administrator to Combat Infantry—he was finally where he wanted to be. He arrived at his new unit at Ft. Lewis, which was deployed in 2009. Adam and his new unit 5-2 Stryker Unit 4/23 Charlie Company were deployed to Afghanistan.

Adam came home for a brief visit in the fall of 2009 and returned in November. He spent the next few months in various military missions for his unit. Early on the morning of February 9, 2010, Adam and two other soldiers were clearing a culvert when they were attacked with an IED. Adam died from his wounds. We never got to hear his voice again.

Adam loved to hug and he was a great hugger. Everyone who ever met Adam remarked on what a genuine, loving person he was. When I met some of his friends from his unit, I was told from one young man that there were three separate times he was pinned down under fire and Adam came back and pulled him to safety. I was told of another time Adam rescued a dog that some Afghans were hurting. Others told me of Adam's ability to make everyone laugh. His commander told me that when he arrived as a new commander of the unit, Adam came to his tent and challenged him to a game of basketball. He said Adam was attempting to put a nervous officer at ease, while making him feel welcomed. I was told Adam didn't care about rank when it came to friendship. He cared about each and every man there.

Adam was a loving, caring, brave, funny young man. He loved everyone and everyone loved him. I do not know anyone who had anything negative to say about my brave son. Adam is my hero. I was told that one of the last things he said to the doctor was to let him call his Mom, "because she is going to be mad that I got hurt and I have to explain things to her." Even in his final moments, Adam was worried about me.

In Memory of Capt. Russell Rippetoe
7/21/1975-4/3/2003
Killed in a suicide car bombing

Home City and State: Denver, CO
Military Branch/Unit: Company A, 3rd Battalion, 75th Ranger Regiment, U.S. Army
Dates Served: 10/1/2001-4/3/2003
Tour of Duty: Operation Iraqi Freedom

Biography and Memories shared by Lesley Spradlin, Proud Best Friend
There was never a time Russell could turn down an opportunity to rush in to rescue someone. Whether it was someone who had gotten into a situation he couldn't handle, a friend who needed a special date to the prom, or a stranger who needed help, Russ was always the knight in shining armor. While we all loved this trait, it's hard knowing this trait is what spurred him to run to the help of a pregnant Iraqi woman, who accompanied the bomb that would end his life. But I don't think any of us would have wanted Russell to be any different. His "knight in shining armor" trait blessed my life in more ways than I can count. It made Russell . . . Russell. And, that's who we loved.

I have so many favorite "Russell moments," it's hard to pick just one. Russ and I were high school sweethearts, and then we dated on and off through college. For college, I moved from Arizona to Colorado. Driving in the snow was foreign to me. The first real snow we got that year, I was working late at night—a 45-minute drive from my dorm room. Lo and behold, I go to my car after my shift ends and there's Russell with a broom, dusting off my car. I didn't even have an ice scraper!

Russ had me follow him as he drove all the way to my dorm—making tracks for me in the road and watching me in his rear view mirror the entire way. He made the hour-long drive to my dorm and then the hour-long drive back to his house—just to make sure I was ok. I don't even think we were dating at that moment in time, but that was just Russell. He didn't care for anyone part-time or halfway—he always loved with everything he had.

Russell and I were high school sweethearts and dated on and off for nine years. He was my best friend. He knew me better than I knew myself in many ways back then.

In Memory of Lance Cpl. Thomas Edward Rivers, Jr.
3/19/1988-4/28/2010
Died when a roadside bomb detonated during a mission to prevent the Taliban from firing on Patrol Base Sofla near Now Zad in Helmand Province, Afghanistan

Home City and State: Birmingham, AL
Military Branch/Unit: Company A, 1st Battalion, 2nd Marine Regiment, 2nd Marine Division, II Marine Expeditionary Force, U.S. Marine Corps
Dates Served: 6/11/2007-4/28/2010
Tour of Duty: Operation Enduring Freedom
Locations Served: Camp LeJeune, NC; Iraq; Helmand Province, Afghanistan

Biography and Memories
Thomas wrote in a ninth grade essay, "I've wanted to be a Marine since I was 10 years old. Joining the Marines would be a good experience because it would help me to rely on God to make it through."

Thomas wrote in his journal that he knew God called him to be a warrior. There was never any doubt. Thomas struggled in school until his recruiter told him he needed a diploma and must graduate to enlist in the Marines. After that conversation, motivation and low grades were not a problem. Thomas graduated May 2007 and fulfilled his dream by joining the Marines two weeks later.

On April 28, 2010, while leading his team to guard a shelled-out building, Thomas ordered his men to take their positions. The Marine ordered to stand security watch was exhausted, so Thomas told him to rest; he would stand post for him. As Thomas walked to the designated area, he triggered an IED.

Thomas had given his heart to his Lord Jesus Christ and his life for his country. Greater love has no one than this that one lay down his life for his friends (John 15:13).

Thomas's mother's favorite moment with her son was when she took him to a Christmas program at a local church. The performance clearly showed what happens to those who die and do not know Jesus. He was only about 10 years old and, being small for his age, the ushers tried to take him to the nursery. Thomas was very mature; he listened and watched intensely. At the end, he walked to the front to confirm his faith in his Lord Jesus Christ. Charon, his mother, lost sight of her young son and was scared but very proud that he had taken a stand for his faith. That is something he would do later in life, as he did that night.

Thomas's father recalls many enjoyable moments he shared with his son. Among the best memories included hunting and scuba diving. One particularly memorable trip includes a very difficult dive, where several more experienced divers returned to the dive boat unable to complete the three excursion dives. Even though it was only Thomas's second open water dive, he enjoyed it and completed all the dives without complaint.

Thomas was the only son of Tom and Charon Rivers. He is also survived by his sister Rachel. The family has remained strong in their faith. The story of his death has changed many lives. The Rivers family knows that, one day, they will join Thomas in their Heavenly home.

Chapter 3

S through Z

Memoirs of fallen soldiers listed alphabetically by last name

In Memory of Sgt. Kenneth John Schall
6/27/1982-5/22/2005
Killed in a Humvee accident in Yusafiyah, Iraq

Home City and State: Peoria, AZ
Military Branch/Unit: Company A, 2nd Battalion, 70th Armor
    Regiment, 3rd Brigade, 1st Armored Division, U.S. Army
Dates Served: 5/20/2003-5/22/2005
Tour of Duty: Operation Iraqi Freedom
Locations Served: Iraq

Biography and Memories
Kenny was the oldest child of John and Terri Schall; brother to
Jessica and Matthew; brother-in-law to Scott; and uncle to Ethan.

His passion in life was golf. In fact, he was attending Glendale
Community College on a partial golf scholarship, where he was
studying to become a high school history teacher. Then, 9/11
happened. That fateful day changed his life, and his family's,
forever. He lived his life to the fullest every day. He loved to fish and
snowboard with friends. His smile and laughter were infectious. And,
whenever he walked into a room, people would gravitate toward him.

He is missed and loved by so many. Every day with Kenny provided
memories that we will all cherish forever!

In Memory of Cpl. Christopher Franklin Sitton
6/1/1982-8/19/2006
One of three soldiers killed when a roadside bomb detonated near
their vehicle while traveling in a convoy to Korengal Outpost in the
Korengal Valley of Kunar Province, Afghanistan

Home City and State: Montrose, CO
Military Branch/Unit: 710th Combat Support Battalion, 3rd
    Brigade Combat Team, 10th Mountain Division, U.S. Army

Dates Served: 1/1/2004-8/19/2006
Tour of Duty: Operation Enduring Freedom
Locations Served: Afghanistan

Biography and Memories
Chris was born in Quinlan, TX to Steve and Judy Sitton. He had one sister, Laura Sitton. Chris was a cheerful, energetic young man who made the most of every single day. He excelled in sports and loved music of all genres. He played the trumpet in his high school marching band and jazz band. He was an Eagle Scout, life guard, and a standout member of the track team.

Chris's father, Steve, was a volunteer firefighter in Texas, and Chris grew up riding to calls with his dad. It was this experience that encouraged Chris to sign on as a combat medic when he enlisted in the Army. He took his job very seriously and dedicated himself to caring for the lives and well-being of his fellow soldiers. Chris and a fellow medic were killed when their Humvee was hit by an IED in the Kunar Valley.

Chris is remembered for having a smile the size of Texas. He was a friend, leader, mentor, and loving son and brother. These are the words used to describe Chris by those who knew and loved him.

Chris served on funeral detail when he was stationed at Ft. Drum, NY. During Chris's memorial service, the soldier who worked funeral detail with Chris told his mother a story of a trip the two took to New York City. They went to Ground Zero and visited the church that survived the terrorist attack. The soldier said Chris stretched out on a pew and reflected upon the events of Sept 11, 2001. At first, the soldier thought Chris was being cocky, but then realized how touched with emotion Chris was. Chris told him, "If only I could have been there that day, I could have helped the injured and maybe saved someone, or assisted with triage." The soldier was touched by Chris's dedication to his duty. The Sittons are so proud of our son. He is missed.

In Memory of Staff Sgt. Trevor L. Spink, Jr.
11/22/1967-7/10/2004
Killed in a vehicle accident in Anbar province, Iraq

Home City and State: Farmington, MO
Military Branch/Unit: 3rd Battalion, 1st Marine Regiment, 1st
   Marine Division, 1st Marine Expeditionary Force, U.S. Marines
   Corps
Dates Served: 1986-2004
Tour of Duty: Operation Iraqi Freedom

Biography and Memories shared by Pam Oder, Proud Mother
Trevor was a Boy Scout, Eagle Scout, and was in the Law
Enforcement Explorer program when he was in high school. Trevor
was always cheerful, courteous and helpful, even as a child. He
was a dedicated Marine and was proud to serve our country. Trevor
resigned a desk job, and requested to be deployed with "his men"
in infantry. That was his second tour of duty in Iraq. We lost him on
his third tour.

Trevor was chosen from several hundred Marines to be the "poster
boy" for the Marine Corps; he was in magazines and on posters and
billboards throughout the United States from 1996-2000.

Trevor loved to joke and play pranks on people. He called me
from Okinawa one evening and said he had been selected to be on
billboards to represent the USMC. I waited for the punch line but
he wasn't joking! When the representative from the photography
studio spoke with me, he told me to be prepared when I saw the
first billboard. I definitely was not prepared; I got goose bumps
and teared up when I saw my son on that billboard in his uniform.

Trev was in Okinawa for three more months after the billboards
started appearing, so he didn't get to see one until he came to visit
Bob and me in Las Vegas (there were at least three billboards in
Vegas).

It takes a special type of person to serve our country. They all know they may have to give their lives to keep us safe and allow us to have our freedom. God bless our troops. God bless all who are involved in this effort to remember our fallen heroes. God bless the United States of America.

In Memory of Spc. Jared Donald Stanker
10/13/1987-10/27/2009
Died in Arghandab Valley, Afghanistan, of wounds suffered when enemy forces attacked his vehicle with a makeshift bomb

Home City and State: Evergreen Park, IL
Military Branch/Unit: 1st Battalion, 17th Infantry Regiment, 5th Stryker Brigade Combat Team, 2nd Infantry Division, U.S. Army
Dates Served: 11/6/2006-10/27/2009
Tour of Duty: Operation Iraqi Freedom
Locations Served: Ft. Lewis, WA; Kandahar, Afghanistan; Arghandab Valley, Afghanistan

Biography:
Jared joined the Army on October 13, 2006, his 18th birthday. He reported to Ft. Benning, GA, on November 2, 2006. Upon completing Basic Training on March 7, 2007, he reported to Ft. Lewis, WA, to join the newly formed 5-2 Stryker Brigade, 1/17 INF Charlie Company, where he became a skilled Stryker driver.

In July 2009, he deployed to Afghanistan with his unit under Operation Enduring Freedom. On October 27, 2009, while on a dismounted mission in the Arghandab River Valley, his Stryker was attacked by an IED. Jared, Sfc. Luis Gonzalez, Sgt. Isaac Jackson, Sgt. Dale Griffin, Sgt. Fernando DeLaRosa, Sgt. Patrick Williamson, Pfc Christoper Walz, and their interpreter Mohammed Nasiry were killed.

Memories shared by Susan Stanker, Proud Mother:
There are way too many moments to list them all. But, my favorite moments—the ones I think about most—are his homecomings. I will always remember seeing Jared come down the escalator at the airport and, at that moment, our eyes making contact. I will forever remember his big bear hug and his immediate need to have a cigarette! Once home, we would go right out on the balcony, play his music on his laptop, and proceed to tell me all of his Army stories and show me his pictures. Jared made me laugh so hard. He was so proud of his accomplishments and of the soldiers in his unit. I loved our "mother and son time" and enjoyed just the two of us catching up.

In Memory of 1ˢᵗ Lt. Andrew Karl Stern
3/28/1980-9/16/2004
Died from injuries received due to enemy action in Anbar Province, Iraq

Home City and State: Germantown, TN
Military Branch/Unit: Company B, 1st Tank Battalion, 1st Marine
    Division, I Marine Expeditionary Force, U.S. Marine Corps
Dates Served: 10/4/2002-9/16/2004
Tour of Duty: Operation Iraqi Freedom
Locations Served: AOBC Ft. Knox, KY; Twenty Nine Palms, CA;
    Fallujah, Iraq

Biography and Memories
Andy Stern was born on March 28, 1980, and spent his youth in suburban Chicago. Andy attended high school at Culver Academy in Indiana, where he co-captained the crew team and achieved the second highest rank among 700 men.

Andy was a business graduate of the University of Tennessee (UT). At UT, he captained the rowing team and enrolled in the Marine Platoon Leaders Program. Andy accepted his Commission on December 15, 2001-the day he graduated from college.

Andy graduated from the Marine Basic School in Quantico, VA, in 2003, ranking 13th in a class of 236 officers. Later in 2003, he graduated from Armor Officer School at Ft. Knox, KY, where he became a Tank Platoon Commander, ranking third in a class of 64. Andy was promoted to 1st Lieutenant in December. Then, in April 2004, Andy took command of the four tanks and 16 men in the 3rd Platoon, Bravo Company, 1st Tank Battalion. Andy left for Iraq on April 17. During seven days in August 2004, his platoon was involved in intense fighting. They completed many missions without incurring injuries. For leadership, gallantry and courage during this period, Andy was awarded a Bronze Star with Valor. On September 16, the platoon was providing security near Fallujah. An engineer asked Andy to inspect debris. Andy saw a concealed IED, and used his body to shield his gun loader, saving the man's life. Andy took shrapnel to the face and neck; he died four hours later. Andy now rests at Arlington National Cemetery. On October 8, 2004, 22 days after he was killed, all 15 men in his platoon returned home.

In Memory of Sgt. Philip J. Svitak
5/21/1970-3/4/2002
Svitak, a gunner on a MH-47 Chinook helicopter, was shot and killed as his helicopter landed on Takur Ghar mountain in eastern Afghanistan to rescue a Navy SEAL who was under fire from al Qaeda fighters, during Operation Anaconda on March 4, 2002. He was one of seven U.S. servicemen killed in the battle.

Home City and State: Joplin, MO
Military Branch/Unit: Company A, 2nd Battalion, 160th Special Operations Aviation Regiment, U.S. Army
Dates Served: Unknown-3/4/2002
Tour of Duty: Operation Enduring Freedom

Biography
Phil enlisted as a helicopter repairman in 1989 after graduating from Fremont High School in Nebraska. After leaving the Army in 1994, he returned in 1998. He logged more than 150 hours of

combat flight time during missions in Afghanistan before he was killed. He was an avid cyclist, and especially loved mountain biking. During his last tour of duty, two MH-47 Chinook helicopters were struck by enemy fire in the Shahikot mountain area. One soldier died when he fell off the first helicopter, and six others were killed after the second Chinook landed in an attempt to rescue him.

Memories Shared by Roseann Svitak, Proud Mother
When he was young, many a time Phil tried our patience with the stunts he pulled. So, we were hard on him and we definitely had our hands full trying to mold him into someone decent that society would respect and accept with open arms.

We have letters from when he was at boot camp stating that he was glad we had been hard on him because, compared to us, boot camp was a "cake walk." Our dreams and our goals for our son were that he would grow up to be responsible, honorable, honest, caring, independent, respectful of others, and the list goes on.

Somewhere along the way (thanks to the help of many family members and friends), Phil managed to attain all of these goals and many more. He was respected by his peers. He was a wonderful husband and a loving daddy. His boys worshipped him.

I do not know when he changed from that "imp with the grin" into the man so many grew to respect, but I will always be grateful that he became a person we can always be proud of, and that our collective efforts weren't "aught for naught."

Some of my most precious memories are of Phil in his youth. His father Richard ran a Jewel Tea Route. Three days of each week, he was "out of town," either to Columbus or Norfolk, NE. Constantly, I thought of the song "Cats in the Cradle" and I wanted Phil to have more exposure to his dad—I often took him to stay overnight with his dad. As we drove down the road, Phil would read to me—he loved books. But my favorite part of those drives was when I would reach over and take his small hand in mine and we would play "Squeeze Squeeze." I would squeeze his hand and tell him I loved him; then, he would squeeze mine and say, "I love you, too, mommy." To some, it may seem just a small gesture, and yet I logged this memory among moments I treasure the most.

Phil loved to hide from us. When he was about two, we bought Rich a roll top desk that dismantled completely for easier transportation from one location to another. We had been assembling it in our living room, but we stopped for some reason or another. Later, when we returned to our task, we discovered our child missing!! We called his name and commenced to search every nook and cranny in our home. Our efforts proved fruitless and we simply could not find him. Where can a munchkin hide in a small two bedroom house? That question was answered when we heard him giggling with joy; he had found a new hidey hole in the desk where the bottom drawer belonged. This was not the first time this little rascal played "heart failure hide and seek" with us.

We had a home on "Green Acres" in Lincoln, NE near Pioneers Park on Coddington Street, up the hill from Lee's Restaurant (they had THE BEST chicken!!). We had an extremely overprotective white German Shepherd female named "Sugarlass" who loved Phil with her whole heart. "Sugar" had three pups and Phil loved being outside playing with them. One day, when Phil was about five, that whole "ball of wax" just totally disappeared. I was frantic and looked all over for them. "Sugar" never left Philip's side. Where would she go with him and three mid-size pups? I went to neighbors and all over. Then, after heading back home, again, I checked the dog house on the back patio (it was NOT a very large dog house). Lo and behold, when I looked in the door all I saw were eyes, elbows and "backsides." To this day, I don't know how they all fit in that dog house, nor how they stayed in there for the length of time it took me to search for them, nor how he managed to keep them so quiet during the times I passed by.

Another memory brings laughter . . . We lived about four blocks away from Richard's younger brother Rainold "Ray" Svitak, his wife Betty, and their children Jeff and Misty. Often, Phil would just wander over there and when I would go to retrieve him, I would see a car in Ray's driveway with the hood up and a pair of "man legs" and body hanging over one fender. On the other fender, an abbreviated set of "kid legs" with feet dangling. I wouldn't see Phil at first because he was under the hood sitting on the engine of the car, assisting and learning all the mechanics and "man points" his mind could absorb. The sight of those two sets of legs hanging from under the hood just struck me as hilarious.

Two very fond memories I have of Phil when he was about 13 involve the time he worked for Dekalb cutting "suckers" from the base of corn stalks. One afternoon when he returned from the fields, he was really upset and I asked him what was bothering him. He told me that one of the older boys in a lead position had pushed a smaller boy face down in the mud because he was slower than the rest of the crew. Phil and the other boys were told not to say or do anything. I am glad Phil brought the matter to my attention because he had a soft heart and he wanted this injustice attended to. We called Dekalb and spoke to the foreman there-the bullying stopped immediately.

When Phil received his first paycheck from Dekalb, he told me he was taking me "out to dinner." He took me to Brestwood—they had a wonderful buffet set out at lunch time. He was the perfect gentleman—he opened the door to the restaurant for me, he escorted me to a table and even pulled my chair out for me so I could get seated comfortably. After an excellent meal, the waitress brought the ticket and almost made the mistake of giving it to me. Phil immediately told her that he was paying for the meal. He left a tip on the table for her; then, as we exited the restaurant, it was deeply touching to watch him go up to the cashier, take out his billfold and pay for that tab. I realized my son was growing up—I think faster than I wanted.

Then there was the rocket . . . I have no idea where he got the instructions on how to build that rocket, but he got them. First, Phil started badgering Rich for one of Rich's large slick sales cards so he could make a Rocket Launcher Tube. Once our mini-genius had his launcher tube, the only thing lacking was the battery to give it its boost. We were not wealthy, so it took a bit before we mustered up the funds to get the large square battery he required to complete his launcher. My parents had come for a visit, so they had their motor home parked in our driveway. We owned a large, older two-story Victorian-style home with an attic, so it stood pretty tall. Phil told his Grandpa that he may want to move the motor home to the lots to the west of the house as he thought it would be safer over there. I'm thinking, "Safer over there? What the heck?" You can't even begin to imagine our disbelief when Phil powered up his rocket and sent that puppy clear over the house, across the street, and into the lots we owned to the north of our home. Our mouths dropped open. I still have that rocket and the memory remains strong.

We moved from our Lincoln home to acreage near Valley, NE. Phil enjoyed the "farm" life. We put in a huge garden. While we planted and attended to our garden, Phil planted his own small garden. We carefully measured distance and depth—he tossed seeds into holes he dug. Our garden did okay, but his garden flourished. Highway 36 ran directly in front of our house and there was a lot of traffic that used the highway. Phil said he wanted to sell some of his vegetables and melons to earn some money. So, he loaded up his wagon and took it up to the mailbox and commenced to join the "job ranks." One day he made over $14 in a very short period of time and he was overjoyed. His money was his own and he hoarded it.

Phil was a member of the Civil Air Patrol in Fremont, along with his best friends Shannon Stone and Eric Ulven. He really enjoyed being a cadet and would stay after hours chatting with Col. Kuddas. Phil and Shannon (I am unsure about Eric) earned the Billy Mitchell Award, the highest award cadets can earn.

When we went to Ft. Campbell to visit Phil he loved taking us on base to show us the "Night Stalker" compound. He had extreme pride in his unit (the 160th), and his beret which announced to "those in the know" that he was a member of a Special Forces Unit. He was also proud of his abilities to take care of the big Chinook

Helicopters. His dream was to become a pilot and fly them. He took us to Fox Hangar and gave us a tour of "HIS" Helicopter. He knew that beast front to back, top to bottom, inside and outside, and he loved it. Another spot that he took us to was the Night Stalker monument, where names of his friends who had been killed were etched. He would spend several moments with his head bowed in prayer for those who had died. Little did he know that, in the not too distant future, his name would accompany theirs on that wall of fame. Phil died doing what he wanted to do—what he loved to do—attempting to perform a search and rescue effort for a fellow American.

Memories shared by family and friends

Dear Philip, it saddens me to think of you as a fallen soldier. You may not be here with us but I promise you, you'll live forever in our hearts and minds. You'll always be an American Hero, just as were your mom, dad, uncles, cousins, and friends who have served before you.

I have many good memories of you as you grew and matured into a young man. I remember you coming over in the mornings to catch a ride to school and how you were so excited the day you jumped on your pogo stick all the way to our house without falling once.

Those skate board ramps and bicycle jumps you built in your back yard were really cool, too. And, you were the first person I ever saw "cooking" bugs collected from a bug zapper!

You especially loved Halloween and looked so cute with your white thermal underwear stuffed with pillows transforming you into the Pillsbury Dough Boy. Another year, you had purple balloons pinned to your clothes making you into a "bunch of grapes." The only problem was, you couldn't sit down without popping balloons. And, remember when you and Jeff wore those spooky monster masks and scared the dickens out of our cat!?

Your bicycle was your main mode of transportation for several years and, when I saw you on your bike, I mostly just saw a cloud of dust and spitting gravel. Then, as you grew older and into cars, all I could see was your and Uncle Ray's backsides sticking out from under the hood as you worked non-stop getting that Firebird's engine to purr.

You were quite a kid with that impish little grin and I sure wish you would have had the opportunity to see your sons grow up. You would have had so many great adventures and shared special memories with them as well.

We were proud of you when you joined the military; we marveled at your accomplishments. We were so concerned for your safety, we prayed for you daily. The last letter I sent to you in Afghanistan was returned to me, unopened, stamped "Return to Sender." Someday, I will hand deliver it to you.
Betty Svitak, Proud Aunt

In Memory of Lance Cpl. John Joshua Thornton
11/19/1983-2/25/2006
Died of wounds received as a result of an enemy mortar attack in Ar Ramadi, Iraq

Home City and State: Phoenix, AZ
Military Branch/Unit: Company K, 3rd Battalion, 7th Marine Regiment, 1st Marine Division, I Marine Expeditionary Force, U.S. Marine Corps
Dates Served: 10/31/2005-2/25/2006
Tour of Duty: Operation Iraqi Freedom
Locations Served: Ar Ramadi, Iraq

Biography
John (Josh) grew up in Phoenix, AZ. He was raised by his mother and Alvarado grandparents after his father passed away. Josh was a very athletic person, who was interested in karate, kickboxing, baseball, soccer, and many other sports.

As a young child, he worked his way up to a second degree black belt. He was one of the youngest children to receive the second degree black belt. He not only enjoyed learning new sports and activities, but he enjoyed and thrived on teaching other kids karate. He taught underprivileged children karate at Fowler Elementary School.

Memories shared by Rachel Thornton, Proud Mother
Besides being such a sweet person, Josh had a heart for his country and being a hero. Since he was a child, Josh dreamed of becoming a Marine.

One of my favorite moments with my son was probably when I would drive him, along with my two other children, to karate lessons. John would usually have a playful mood after practice, and the other two were typically worn out. But John didn't mind; he was always trying to have fun. Usually he would yank on his sister's hair or make silly faces at my other son. Whatever he was doing, apparently, it was behind my back and, honestly, I never witnessed it. But those rides home were the best. They were the best because those were the times we spent together—just me and my three kids. Regardless if they were gnawing on each other's heads, we were all together. That is something we all dearly miss.

Memories shared by family and friends
John was my oldest brother. Before the cammies were crisply ironed and the boots were laced up high, he was known as the nicest, most caring, loveable guy in Phoenix. For any problems or dilemmas, John always had the right words to say to make matters better.

Not only was John nice and caring, he was one the funniest people I have ever spoken to. He knew exactly how to turn anybody's day from a negative one to the best day ever. I'm not sure how he got that sense of humor, but everyone who knew John knew him by his caring personality, wise humor and his slanted yet so perfect smile.

Almost every day with John was the best time ever. To narrow it down, I'll try and pick a funny moment. Well, it's funny now, but it was one of the most intense moments we ever shared. One day John was just pushing my buttons and annoying the life out of me. I remember him using that wise humor against me, along with my other brother Kyle. To make a long story short, I was eating cereal and they were just there being little pests joking about me. I got tired and I threw my cereal, milk and all, right at John's face. Oh my goodness, I ran away from him so fast; but, he caught me and I was in so much trouble that day it was unreal. Yet, to look back on that day is remarkable.

Brianna Thornton, Proud Sister

My name is Gil Contreras and I am a Marine. I retired in August of 2004 after 21-and-a-half years of service. I spent my last two years assigned to 3d Battalion, 11th Marines out of Twentynine Palms, CA, where Josh was assigned. I was also assigned to 7th Marine Regiment during the war, the same Regiment Josh was assigned.

I did not have the pleasure of serving with Josh, nor did I ever meet him. When his Uncle John called and asked me if I would do Josh's eulogy, I had a number of emotions that hit me all at once. First off, I was honored, then embarrassed and saddened. I immediately said yes. I sat alone and asked myself, "What will I say about this young Marine that will do him justice? What did he do for fun? What made him happy? How did he feel about the war and the men he fought with? What was his family like? What right did I have to speak about this young Marine?"

John Joshua Thornton was born on November 19, 1983 in Phoenix, Arizona to Rachel and Robert Thornton. He grew up in the Phoenix area with his brother Kyle and sister Brianna. He attended Tolleson High School, where he was part of the ROTC Program and graduated in 2002. He stayed in the area upon graduation and held down a few miscellaneous jobs until November 1, 2004, when he joined the United States Marine Corps.

I made a few phone calls to various Marine units to see if I could speak with friends of this young Marine so they could tell me about him.

As doors slowly began to open I kept hearing the same theme, as noted by First Sergeant Smith who was there with Josh in Ar Ramadi, where he fell to an enemy mortar:

Lance Corporal Thornton would always smile, even in the worst of conditions. He was a Marine who was easy to like. He was a real laid back kind of guy who never judged his fellow Marine. He was very good at drawing and was always sketching something. You could wake him up after he did not sleep for days and he would gladly cut your hair. He would often tell stories and make you laugh. He really enjoyed getting tattoos and he had a talent for sketching them. Josh carried the radio because he was strong and could communicate well with higher command. He will always be remembered for his ability to smile, in every circumstance, and his willingness to always help fellow Marines. Lance Corporal Thornton will be greatly missed, but not forgotten.

I asked Josh's Uncle John if I could meet his family and walk in Josh's bedroom. He said yes and when I arrived I was greeted by John and introduced to Josh's wonderful family.

Josh was a rich man, not in the monetary sense, but in the spiritual sense. He has a strong, beautiful and caring mother who is the center of the family at this time. He also has a younger brother who idolized his older brother and a beautiful, younger sister who had to put up with both of them.

Friends and family were present and I was introduced to them as they came and went to pay their respects to Rachel and her family. I looked at a number of photos of Josh through various stages of his life and then we finally walked down the hall to his room. As I entered, I immediately found what I was looking for . . . he was guilty. He is a TRUE MARINE. Every wall, every piece of furniture had Marine Corps paraphernalia on it. Through the hundreds of skateboarding stickers on his closet I found a Marine Corps sticker, photo of the Battle at Belleu Wood in 1918, and a Marine Corps Drill Instructor photo. On his dresser were numerous stuffed animals that were all camouflaged, as well as an inert hand grenade. Rachel told me all he wanted to be was a Marine Rifleman! On every wall in Josh's room there was the cornerstone of what the Corps bases its foundation of leadership, as well as pictures of Christ and various religious medallions. God, Country and Corps . . . Josh lived it well before he became a Marine.

I left the house and went to Tolleson High School to meet with his ROTC instructors. We spoke about Josh and reminisced about our times as Marines. Embellishing a few sea stories and, of course, talking about Josh, the scholarship fund being developed in his name, and where his photo will be placed for all to see and remember why America is free. The Colonel is a hardened Vietnam Veteran, Master Gunnery Sergeant, and a Desert Storm era Marine.

Channel 12 News reporter Sylest Rodriguez was present. She was doing a story on Josh and asked my relationship to him. I read her the following article written by Martin Savidge, a CNN reporter who was embedded with the 7th Marine Regiment during the start of the war. I did him some favors as we advanced towards Baghdad, so he wrote my wife a letter when he returned telling her I was okay.

His letter is titled, "Young Men Like This":

Martin Savidge of CNN, embedded with the 1st Battalion, 7th Marines, was talking with four young Marines near his fighting hole this morning live on CNN. He had been telling the story of how well the Marines had been looking out for and taking care of him since the war started. He went on to tell about the many hardships the Marines had endured since the war began and how they all look after one another. He turned to the four and said he had cleared it with their commanders and they could use his video phone to call home. The 19-year-old Marine next to him asked Martin if he would allow his platoon sergeant to use his call to call his pregnant wife back home, whom he had not been able to talk to in three months.

A stunned Savidge, who was visibly moved by the request, shook his head and the young Marine ran off to get the sergeant. Savidge recovered after a few seconds and turned back to the three young Marines still sitting with him and asked which one of them would like to call home first. The Marine closest to him responded without a moment's hesitation, "Sir, if it's all the same to you we would like to call the parents of a buddy of ours, Lance Corporal Brian Buesing of Cedar Key, FL, who was killed on March 23, 2003, near An-Nasiriya to see how they are doing." Martin Savidge totally broke down and was unable to speak. All he could get out before signing off was, "Where do they get young men like this?"

I tell you, they get them from Phoenix, AZ, and families who support them encourage them to live out their dreams, regardless of the cost, based on a simple principle that fighting and dying for this country is worth it. These warriors like Lance Corporal Thornton, mostly young, all volunteers are prepared to give their lives for our future, the future of his younger brother and sister, as well as a people he didn't even know.

He carried the weight of the world on his shoulders while he was a Marine. Not concerned with politics or the reason he was told he must fight. He had to make some tough decisions just to survive, which I am sure haunted his memories as he would not share these demons with others. Many times they were disguised with tough words, but he always carried the love of his family and fellow Marines in his heart; he would not let them down. This I believe in my heart, he was true to being, "No better friend, and no worse enemy . . . A UNITED STATES MARINE!"

I would like to thank the Lord for giving Josh to us for his short 22 years than to have never been given him at all. I ask that all of you who read this, get down on your knees tonight and pray that we all love each other and share Josh and the others you have read about in this book with everyone you come in contact with. We should live our lives with a smile, just as they have done in the worst of conditions.

God Bless you all and Semper Fidelis.

In Memory of 1st Lt. Matthew Vandegrift
4/17/1980-4/21/2008
Killed while conducting combat operations in Basra, Iraq

Home City and State: Littleton, CO
Military Branch/Unit: 2nd Battalion, 10th Marine Regiment, 2nd Marine Division, 2nd Marine Expeditionary Force, U.S. Marine Corps
Dates Served: Unknown-4/21/2008
Tour of Duty: Operation Iraqi Freedom

Matthew Vandegrift with his mother Mary Jane.

Biography and Memories

Matthew graduated from high school near Austin, TX in 1999, where he was an exceptional student and talented athlete. He graduated from Texas A&M a few years later, again, with honors. A knee ligament injury stood in the way of Matt joining the Marines. He underwent surgery and months of physical therapy, all with the desire to survive the rigors of the recruit physical. He achieved this goal and was accepted into the Marines in 2005. In 2007, Matt left for Iraq as an infantry officer. In April of this 2008, he gave the ultimate sacrifice on our behalf when he was killed in action. The Leander School district in Texas voted unanimously to name their new high school, opened in 2010 after him.

John Vandegrift, Proud Father

Matt Vandegrift was an honor student who exemplified the ethical behaviors that we teach and model for our students. In addition, he volunteered to defend you and me—and our nation—dying in this service. We, too, are proud of Matt. He will serve as an inspiration and role model for future Vandegrift High School students. I believe that Vandegrift High School is a name that will inspire our young people, and a worthy choice.

Proud Superintendent of Leander School district, home of Vandegrift High School

Matt would never have asked, or probably cared, that a school be named after him. Being the kind of guy he was, his sacrifice was for all of us and the ideals we believe in, not for self aggrandizement. And not only for us, but also for the Iraqi people, who he was training to defend themselves. Many times talking to him, he said that they were making good progress in standing up on their own, and that he had hope that eventually we'd be able to leave them to defend themselves. Anyway, he was so much more than just another uniform. His love and bright character will not be soon forgotten by those who knew him.
Barrett Vandegrift, Proud Brother

When I first met Matt, I was immediately impressed with his character. Anyone who had ever been acquainted with him will probably tell you that he was one of the most well-rounded individuals you would ever know. Matt was a brilliant individual, who seemed to have a thorough knowledge on everything. Whether we were discussing proper dieting, current events around the world, or what state has the best BBQ, he would provide you with factual details and by the end of the conversation, he would have you completely convinced and supporting his argument or position on the topic. Most of our teammates would try to challenge him, daily, and debate with him on various things. We would usually find ourselves losing the debate, but also learning something from Matt. In my opinion, Matt's intellect and superior thinking were his greatest attributes. He was a person who was dedicated to academic excellence. But, it was not until after his death that I would learn how far his commitment had taken him. He successfully graduated high school and a prestigious Division I University with honors. When he entered the Marine Corps, he graduated his military occupational school number one, above all Army and Marine Corps lieutenants, which was said to be one of the most challenging entry level schools for commissioned officers. Through his list of accomplishments, Matt always found time to enjoy the things he liked to do, whether it was playing his favorite video games, watching his favorite movies or listening to some good old eighties music. This is one of the things I've learned from him and have applied to my own life—work hard at the things that you want to accomplish, but enjoy life and don't take yourself so seriously that you cannot find pleasure in the things that make you happy.

The last thing I am going to mention about Matt changed my outlook on life—his dedication to his country and the ones he loved. Matt was a man of honor and valor. Although we did not go around saying, "I love you," his actions said it all. In Basra, Iraq, Matt positioned his vehicle in between me and an enemy sniper, who was taking shots at me. Matt called in Army air support to destroy a determined enemy. At the end of the day, Matt put his life in danger for someone he cared about. That same evening, Matt pulled my tangled body through concertina wire. I was pinned down by enemy gun fire and, once again, he came to my aid. On another occasion, Matt rushed into an Iraqi building to aid and protect a fellow team member, who was pinned down by enemy mortar fire.
Harry Boyd, proudly served with Matt from 2007-2008

Matthew Vandegrift

In Memory of Sgt. Adam Alexander Wilkinson
12/17/1983-2/18/2007
Killed in a Chinook helicopter crash

Home City and State: Colorado Springs, CO
Military Branch/Unit: Company B, 2nd Battalion, 160th Special
  Operations Aviation Regiment, U.S. Army
Dates Served: Served 2003-2007
Tour of Duty: Operation Enduring Freedom
Locations Served: Fort Carson, CO

Adam Wilkinson

In Memory of Lance Cpl. Michael Jason Williams
6/1/1971-3/23/2003
Killed during a battle in Nasiriyah., Iraq

Home City and State: Phoenix, AZ
Military Branch/Unit: 1st Battalion, 2nd Marine Regiment, 2nd
  Marine Expeditionary Brigade, U.S. Marine Corps
Dates Served: 10/19/2001-3/23/2003
Tour of Duty: Operation Iraqi Freedom
Locations Served: Camp LeJeune, NC; Kuwait, Iraq

Biography

Michael was born in Reno, NV, on June 1, 1971. He moved to Phoenix, AZ, at six months of age. He grew up in the desert, and with his older brother he collected snakes, lizards and rocks.

He quit high school in the tenth grade, received his GED and completed two years of college. He started a flooring business, using his artistic abilities to create beautiful floors. In 2001, he gave up his business and joined the U.S. Marine Corps. The events of September 11, 2001 solidified his commitment to his country.

Although 30 years old when he joined the Corps, he put everything he had into his training. Most recruits were at least 10 years his junior, earning Mike the nickname of "old man." Throughout boot camp and up to his death in Iraq, his fellow Marines looked up to him with respect and they admired his commitment. His commanding officer said that if all of his Marines were like Mike, he would be commanding the best unit in the Corps.

He was killed in action in An-Nasiriyah, Iraq on March 23, 2003. He died instantly with others in an AAV when their vehicle exploded as a result of air fire. He was not married and did not have any children, but he had friends from all walks of life. His funeral was held in one of the biggest churches in Phoenix.

Memories shared by Sandra Watson, Proud Mother

Mike summed up his take on life's priorities as, "All that matters in life is one's relationship with God and one's relationship with family." He will be missed and loved by many for a very long time. He is truly one of America's heroes.

During a grueling, long distance run in boot camp that constituted a part of the notorious "Crucible," Mike fractured his foot and ran an additional 14 miles to complete the course. During the run, one of his fellow recruits collapsed, and an exhausted Mike picked him up and carried him the last five miles, fractured foot and all.

In Memory of Spc. James Richard Wolf
5/7/1982-11/6/2003
Killed in a convoy when a makeshift bomb detonated in Mosul, Iraq

Home City and State: Scottsbluff, NE
Military Branch/Unit: Headquarters and Headquarters Company,
    52nd Engineer Battalion, 43rd Area Support Group, U.S. Army
Tour of Duty: Operation Iraqi Freedom

Jamie Wolf's first Nebraska Cornhuskers game

Biography and Memories shared by Chris Wolf, Proud Mother
James (we called him Jamie at home) was born number three out
of four children, in Spokane, WA. He was the only dark haired one
of the bunch, and had his dad's brown eyes. The rest of the kids
were blond with blue eyes, like me. Being number three, Jamie was
always very easy going; he took his own time to do anything and
everything. He smiled all the time, loved sports, Ninja Turtles, and
building things. He was always taking things apart so he could try
and figure out how to put them back together!

Jamie wasn't the best student, but tried very hard. As much as he
wanted to become an engineer, he really struggled with math. He

could work any computer drafting program, which was actually his best class besides choir. He enjoyed singing and was involved in choir and swing choir in high school. He was a great dancer and really shined singing and dancing. His grin was a mile wide as he grew to be almost 6' 6" tall.

Jamie's junior year was a tough one for him; he was really searching for some place to go. He did very poorly in school, and his grades were not good enough for him to stay in the show choirs. It was a struggle for all of us. Then, during the summer before his senior year, he came home and said he wanted to join the Army. He could pursue his dream of becoming an engineer, earn some money to go to college, and see the world.

So in August of 1999, I signed papers allowing him to join the US Army. I still don't regret that, because it gave him a goal and some direction in which to complete his last year of high school.

Basic training took him to Ft. Leonard Wood, MO, and we were there to see him graduate. After completing his Advanced Individual Training, he had 30 days of leave in April, and then he was off to his first assignment in South Korea.

Jamie had a desk job, so we spent many of our evenings in a chat room with him. We really had quite a bit of communication with him. The Army wanted him to stay for another year and even though he enjoyed Korea, he wanted to be stateside. His second choice was Ft. Carson, CO, which is where he ended up. Imagine, of all the Army bases in the US, he ends up being five hours away from us! We were so excited to have him close again. He loved Colorado Springs, with so many different things to do; he loved to fish, camp and be outdoors.

Jamie had warned us that his battalion could be deployed, and when that call came telling us he was leaving, he didn't even have time for us to see him before he left. At that point, that weekend was the worst of my life. It was the weekend just before the President declared war on Iraq. It seemed an eternity before we finally received a letter from him, very short but at least it was something. Communication gradually got better; we sent cards, letters, and packages to him. There were a few emails as well.

Jamie was thrilled to finally be doing what he was trained to do. He was a surveyor, and a good one too. He just always made the best of everything, no matter what the conditions.

When R&R started, Jamie was one of the first ones to be given a chance to go home. It was the best 10 days of my life. We were so happy to have him home. He went back to see his choir teacher, and he liked nothing better than to walk through his high school in his dress uniform to show what he had accomplished.

He went to Lincoln, Nebraska to see two of our other children who were in school. He was very sad he missed our youngest daughter's high school graduation while he was in Iraq, but they made up for time lost, as they had always been close. His trip to Lincoln led him to his first Cornhusker football game, which was such a thrill for him. I remember getting a message on the answering machine, calling from the stadium. He was so excited to be there. We took many of pictures of him with lots of family, and enjoyed every minute he was home. I hated sending him off, but we all knew he had to go back. He had a sense of responsibility to his comrades who were doing his job while he was gone. So with a kiss and a prayer, we said goodbye to him. That was in October of 2003.

On Nov 6, 2003, we were informed of his death. Within an hour, we had two priests and Sister Vera from our church at our house, and countless people who stopped to give us a hug, bring food (oh my the food!), and flowers. Some of these people we didn't even know. That afternoon, we received calls from our son's company commanders, as well as his battalion commander, from Iraq.

Ft. Carson was extremely good to us, treating us with so much love and concern every time we visit. We have become close friends with Jamie's section sergeant, who is a Nebraska boy himself. He and Jamie were very close, and he took Jamie's death so hard. He and his wife had a baby girl less than a month after we lost Jamie, and they named her "Jamie Ann." We were so touched, and this family has become family to us. They are now in Germany, and we miss them terribly.

We Jamie's unit when they came home from Iraq, and were instantly wrapped in their love and support. We met one of the soldiers who was in the vehicle with James; he was not injured. He is such a nice young man and, even though he is out of the Army now, we still stay in touch. We also met the ones who were with our son at the end; he didn't last more than 30 minutes after the bomb went off. He didn't suffer, probably didn't even know what hit him. It gave us a sense of peace knowing there were people around who loved him and did all they could to save him. They answered all of our questions honestly, and did nothing but speak highly of James.

We were honored, again, when the newest dining facility at Ft. Carson was named "The James R. Wolf Dining Facility." We thought it was very appropriate seeing how he ate like a horse. But being as tall as he was, we could never fill him up!

James was part of the 52nd Engineer Battalion. Then he was attached to the 101st Airborne Division in Mosul. He was proud of the fact that they were rebuilding schools, orphanages, and homes. He believed they were doing a good thing over there; the people were very grateful for the work they were doing.

As you can tell, we are very proud of our son, who he was and what he stood for. We decided to keep his Bronco; he had such plans for it. We feel one thing we can do to honor him is to see his plans completed.

In Memory of Pfc. Kelly David Youngblood
7/2/1987-2/18/2007
Died of wounds suffered during combat operations in Ramadi, Iraq

Home City and State: Mesa, AZ
Military Branch/Unit: 3rd Battalion, 69th Armor Regiment, 1st
    Brigade Combat Team, 3rd Infantry Division, U.S. Army
Dates Served: 1/15/2006-2/18/2007
Tour of Duty: Operation Iraqi Freedom
Locations Served: Iraq

Biography and Memories shared by Kristen Simon, Proud Mother
Thank you for the opportunity to talk about the most patriotic kid I
ever knew: my son Kelly Youngblood.

Once when Kelly was in the third grade, he came home upset. I
asked him, "What's wrong?" Kelly replied, "The kid standing next
to me didn't put his hand over his heart when we said the Pledge of
Allegiance." I knew then that I had a true patriot on my hands.

Kelly, like most young kids, enjoyed the occasional sleepover.
During one sleepover I clearly remember receiving a call from
the mother of Kelly's friend. The boys had stayed up all night
digging trenches in the backyard and playing Army. Fortunately,
she laughed and wasn't upset the boys rearranged their landscape. I
received a letter from this family shortly after Kelly's death stating
that they will never forget this wonderful sweet kid, and that they
still have remnants of the trenches to this day.

I also received a letter from Kelly's sixth grade teacher with a copy
of the sixth grade year book page included. The question at the top
of the page asked, "What do you want to be when you grow up?"
Kelly's answer: "A general in the U.S. Army."

Often, on Saturday mornings, I would enjoy the occasional garage
sale with my friends. Kelly would always tag along because he
wanted to look for used Army gear. Kelly often told me, "When I
grow up, I want to be a soldier." I believed him, but kept it in the

back of my mind. There is a difference between a boy playing army and a boy who knew he was born to be a soldier.

In January 2007, I went to Fort Stewart to visit for a week, to help Kelly pack to say goodbye, and to see him off. In the pit of my heart, I feared this would be the last time I would see his beautiful smile and hear his sweet laugh. The week I spent at Fort Stewart was the best week of my life—just the two of us laughing and joking with his friends, Kelly showing me around the base and introducing me to some of his leaders.

Kelly was killed by sniper fire from enemy insurgents just sixteen days after arriving at that horrible place. My worst fears had become reality. Looking at Army captains at the base of my stairs with their hats in their hands is an image that is burned into my memory. The worst nine words I have ever heard, "The United States of America regrets to inform you . . ." However, I've been blessed to hear the four greatest words, "I love you Mom." On, February 18, 2007, I lost my son, my friend; America lost a true American hero and patriot. God bless you, Kelly, and God bless America.

Index

Arranged in alphabetical order by soldiers' last names